PESTO

The Modern Mother Sauce

PESTO
The Modern Mother Sauce

More Than 90 Inventive Recipes That
Start with Homemade Pestos

Leslie Lennox

S
SURREY
BOOKS

AN AGATE IMPRINT

CHICAGO

First edition published May 2019

Printed in China

10 9 8 7 6 5 4 3 2 1   19 20 21 22 23

ISBN-13: 978-1-57284-268-7 (cloth)
ISBN-10: 1-57284-268-7 (cloth)
eISBN-13: 978-1-57284-827-6
eISBN-10: 1-57284-827-8

Art direction and cover design by Morgan Krehbiel
Interior and cover illustrations by Anna Repp

Surrey Books is an imprint of Agate Publishing. Agate books are available in bulk at discount prices. For more information, visit agatepublishing.com.

To my two favorite people in the
world—my husband, Dave, and our
daughter, Hope. Everything is better
with you . . . and pesto, of course!

and

To my mother, Roberta. Watching you
create has been an inspiration that
started long ago and lasts to this day.
Thank you for sharing all your tricks
of the trade with me.

"Two roads diverged in a
wood, and I—I took the one
less traveled by, and that has
made all the difference."
—ROBERT FROST

Contents

Foreword by Linton Hopkins ix

INTRODUCTION
A Sauce for Life 1

CHAPTER 1
The Modern Mother Sauce
(Pesto Basics) 11

CHAPTER 2
Eggs and Toasts 39

CHAPTER 3
Pastas and Pizzas 53

CHAPTER 4
Sandwiches, Paninis, Bruschetta,
and Crostini 77

CHAPTER 5
Appetizers and Small Bites 95

CHAPTER 6
Soups 113

CHAPTER 7
Vegetables 127

CHAPTER 8
Poultry 149

CHAPTER 9
Seafood 163

CHAPTER 10
Beef, Pork, and Lamb 177

Acknowledgments 195
Kitchen Resources 197
Recipe Index 202
Index 205

FOREWORD

by Linton Hopkins

ONE OF MY FONDEST FOOD MEMORIES is coming home from the Peachtree Road Farmers Market with my wife, Gina, and our two children, carrying bags full of Georgia's best seasonal produce and artisan goods—among them, a jar of Hope's Gardens pesto. After tearing off a chunk of freshly baked ciabatta, we ate our way through that jar as we put our treasures away. We've repeated this weekly ritual of friends, family, and food countless times since building the market more than ten years ago with our friends at Saint Philip's Cathedral.

Linton Hopkins is the chef-owner of five Atlanta-area restaurants known for celebrating local produce and community-driven cuisine, including Restaurant Eugene, the flagship establishment he opened with his wife, Gina, and one bottle shop. He is the cofounder of the Peachtree Road Farmers Market, and his curated artisan food menus can be found on Delta Airlines international flights out of Atlanta. In 2012, Linton received the James Beard Foundation's Award for Best Chef in the Southeast.

The market opening took place in the summer of 2007. Through relationships with artisans like Leslie, what began as six vendors—ranging from coffee roasters to farmers and crafters—grew into a bustling sixty-vendor market that soon included her pesto company, Hope's Gardens. The vision for our market, which was grown from years of conversations with farmers, artisans, and community members and a desire to share "good" food, was able to come to life.

As a chef, I believe there is a need to be connected to who we are as people through kinship with soil, animals, and one another—all of which meet at the shared community table. I share a bond with Leslie, her husband, Dave, and their daughter, Hope, in that they, too, need this interconnected good-food world to be in their lives. The good-food world, with its unbridled deliciousness, joy, and sharing, improves who we are, both physically and spiritually. As food entrepreneurs, we share a spirit and understanding of mutual success and failure. By standing together, we help each other weather the inevitable dips and dives of business because in our world, if one of us loses, we all do.

Hope's Gardens pesto found a place not only in our home but also in my professional kitchen. Like Hope's Gardens, I find that pesto can capture the best of a season and become a means of reducing food waste. Leftover vegetable scraps that many toss into the compost are not "waste" at all. With a little coaxing, fresh olive oil, sea salt, and lemon, they can become a first-rate pesto—which, in turn, becomes a garnish on goat cheese with toast or a sauce for iron skillet steak. This "waste" becomes the centerpiece of your good-food table, and memories with family, friends, and food are thus made.

Please take Leslie's recipes and incorporate them into your cooking. Not only will you improve your life with some amazing meals, you'll also be making the world around you a better place. 🌿

INTRODUCTION

A Sauce for Life

Writing this book has been a labor of love—a long labor! For more than ten years, pesto—or "green gold," as we call it in my family—has been my life. Through a mixture of happenstance, grit, and a lot of good eating, my husband, Dave, and I became "pesto-preneurs" in 2007, when we established our company, Hope's Gardens.

Our pesto was born from abundance. In 1999, Dave and I purchased a house in Atlanta. It was a beautiful home, perfect for raising our newborn daughter, Hope, and in the backyard was a long-neglected garden and a decaying 1937 Lord & Burnham greenhouse. The previous tenants had filled the shelter with rusting equipment and old furniture, but we saw it for what it was: an opportunity. With a little elbow grease and a lot of vision, we restored this bedraggled shack back into a lush, thriving greenhouse and cultivated a flourishing basil crop.

We produced pesto for friends and family, and established a small business, named for our daughter. Through the local farmers market, we shared with customers some of our favorite methods for incorporating pesto into pastas, vegetables, and soups, and encouraged generous dollops of it on pizza.

My husband, Dave, and me under the stained glass window that he designed.

I have always loved talking with customers about pesto and how best to use it. I was surprised that many people had no idea what it was. I found myself creating recipes and combinations on the fly and sharing them. Much to my surprise, they worked, and customers would return to share their successes with us. I started to put these ideas down on paper and distribute them to anyone who stopped by our booth for a sample taste of our "green gold." This morphed into an on-demand cookbook

1

in the days before social media. I would print out twenty-five copies before the market and return with zero. It was then that the seed was planted to put all my thoughts and recipes into a cookbook someday. That was over ten years ago, and that seed is at last bearing fruit!

Meanwhile, Hope's Gardens developed a cult following with local foodies, and it picked up distribution through specialty retailers, including Whole Foods Market. Linton Hopkins, a James Beard Award–winning chef of New South cooking (and the author of this book's foreword), incorporated our blend into his cuisine. We had struck green gold.

But the companion of abundance, sadly, is loss. In 2009, a flash flood swept through our greenhouse, our gardens, and our home. Escaping the rising waters with just a few belongings, we lost nearly everything—but not the greenhouse. Though the plants inside were destroyed, the structure itself weathered the storm without so much as a broken window! It looked as though we were going to be planting the garden again from scratch.

Our community of friends, fans, and business partners, however, took some of the sting out of starting over. Through their care and nourishment— spiritual, financial, and culinary—we were able to rebuild better than before. Starting over taught us unique lessons in appreciating essentials and paring down, and through it all, pesto became a powerful metaphor—it's a steadfast base for building and a source of comfort through plenty and through want.

Pesto isn't so much about a particular configuration of ingredients as it is about *making do*. What's seasonal? What tools do I have? What's left over from last night? In the kitchen, making do isn't just resourceful, though that is one benefit. It also encourages creative thinking, improvisation, and flexibility—tools we could all use a little more of. Making do, in fact, can lead to surprising, delicious dishes that couldn't have come about any other way.

When you have pesto on hand, hundreds of possibilities are within your reach, regardless of your skill level as a cook. Whether you're a college student with meager experience or a seasoned chef who grew up flambéing with Julia, you can count on pesto to be a healthy and convenient base for any meal. One day, it can be the starter for homemade vinaigrette and the next, a building block for stick-to-your-ribs lasagna or a romantic Valentine's Day dinner. It's delicious scooped straight

Dave and young Hope preparing one of the garden beds for spring planting.

When you have pesto on hand, hundreds of possibilities are within your reach, regardless of your skill level as a cook.

Selecting fresh lettuce from the greenhouse for a dinner salad.

from a jar or bundled with asparagus in a savory prosciutto hors d'oeuvre. Best of all, it can be tailored to meet any dietary preference or tweaked to complement the ingredients you have on hand. It's a perfect sauce for experimentation, for preparing a small meal for one, or for feeding a crowd.

It's with this idea in mind that I wrote *Pesto: The Modern Mother Sauce*. I take an elastic, waste-not approach to this familiar condiment by offering a template for you to build a personalized pesto to fit your tastes, resources, and dietary needs. Because I feel strongly that cooking should be a pleasure and not a chore, I've chosen recipes that emphasize ease of preparation; in-season, unfussy ingredients; and versatility.

Capturing tried-and-true favorites that Hope's Gardens has shared with customers and friends over the years, this book walks you through the process of creating your own pesto and incorporating it into dozens of meals, from salads to pastas to poultry—and more. The worksheets in the back of the book (see page 199) will let you record your favorite flavor profiles for future reference, allowing you to make your own personal pesto again and again. With pesto, everything just tastes better.

It's my goal that you'll take away from this volume some of the can-do, creative spirit that pesto has offered me. From Hope's Gardens to your kitchen, I hope that you, too, can have pesto as a sauce for life. 🌿

How to Use This Book

THIS BOOK WILL INTRODUCE YOU TO the Hope's Gardens approach of incorporating your personalized pesto into recipes. While I encourage you to experiment to find your own best way of working, I've found a few practices to be helpful in my own kitchen.

Making the pesto sauce in advance of following a longer recipe is one way of streamlining things while cooking so that you won't be juggling multiple recipes at once. Once your pesto is prepared, the rest will come together quickly.

Before starting on a dish, I recommend reading through the recipe from beginning to end *twice* to avoid any unwelcome surprises as you cook. There's nothing worse than getting halfway through a recipe and realizing you've loaned out the baking sheet you need.

In French cooking there is a term, *mise en place*, which translates to "everything in its place." Many chefs, myself included, use a mise en place method in the kitchen, meaning that each ingredient is measured out and ready to go before cooking begins. (For those of you who prefer using a kitchen scale, I have included universal metric conversion charts in the back of this book so your recipes can come out perfect time after time.)

I consider this a good practice, and advise you to have everything—including utensils, pots, and pans—in place before you start the recipe.

Flexibility is the name of the game in this book. There are so many opportunities to use your favorite ingredients, even when I call for mine. For example, when a recipe calls for any creamy dairy product, options are always interchangeable. You can use yogurt, sour cream, crème fraîche, goat cheese, ricotta, or cream cheese.

I often refer to "rustic-style bread." By this I mean an artisan-made bread with a crispy crust and large holes in the crumb. It might have seeds, grains, or dried fruit in it. Use whatever looks good to you.

Likewise, use the vegetables, grains, and proteins *you* prefer. Feel free to tinker and change these recipes to create your own twists. For example, by substituting a different pesto and changing up one or two of the ingredients, you will never have the same dish twice. Also, most recipes can easily be doubled or halved as needed.

My preference throughout the book is to use the freshest and juiciest ingredients. Seize the season's best; if you don't have your own vegetable garden, make a trip to the nearest farmers market. This is what personalizes a pesto and makes these recipes so great. You be the master of yours.

My preference throughout the book is to use the freshest and juiciest ingredients.

All recipes include a measurement of pesto needed; you'll decide what flavor you would like to use. I make recommendations where I see fit; otherwise, I use the generic term "pesto." I have discovered some wonderful surprises by mixing and matching different ingredients that I found fresh at the farmers market or in the refrigerator at home. Be open to your own surprises and discoveries! These discoveries have provided inventive takes on iconic and classic dishes I used to make. They have been modernized, lightened, and elevated to improve on dishes I did not realize could (or should) be improved on.

All that being said, I do have recommendations for basic ingredients based on how the recipes were tested. For best results, follow the shorthand on the next page.

BASIC INGREDIENT RECOMMENDATIONS

Black pepper. Always freshly ground Tellicherry peppercorns. When you grind and use these, you are in control of the texture, and the taste is fresh and pungent. The longer ground pepper sits around, the more flavor and aroma it loses.

Broth. This is a generic term. Use vegetable, chicken, beef, or fish broth, or just water–whatever you have on hand! See page 8 for my easy method for making homemade vegetable broth.

Butter. Always unsalted. Additional salt is required in each recipe, but you'll have control over how much you use.

Citrus juice. Freshly squeezed juice is my choice whenever possible.

Eggs. Always large.

Garlic. Fresh is best. Avoid the green inner germ, which points to the age of the bulb and tastes bitter. If you see it, remove and discard. Throughout the book I caution you to stay close to garlic cooking in a pan, as it can burn quickly. This will change the flavor from sweet and robust to bitter in an instant. So keep your eyes open and nose clear!

Jalapeños. The heat of a jalapeño is in the seeds and membrane. I like heat, but not too much, so know that when I call for these in a recipe, I tested it with the seeds and membrane removed. If you prefer things hotter, keep them in! I have met people who love heat and pop a habanero pepper in their mouth with delight. You decide your fate!

Milk. These recipes were developed using whole milk. You can use another type, but the flavor and texture of the recipe may be affected.

Olive oil. Always extra virgin olive oil, which means that the oil came from the olives' first pressing. This is olive oil at its purest and finest. Oil degrades over time, so be sure to store it in a dark-colored container in a cool, dark place.

Onions. There is so much variety in the onion world. Use your favorite, unless I note otherwise (if one type works particularly well, I'll let you know). My preference is a sweet Vidalia onion, but they are not always available. Feel free to substitute Spanish onions, spring onion, leeks, chives, shallots, or whatever you have at home or see at the market that is seasonal. Each will impart a slightly different allium flavor, which is just fine.

Paprika. I don't specify a type in my recipes–use your favorite. All paprika is made from dried peppers and offers a pop of color, but the different varieties have distinct qualities. Sweet paprika has a mild flavor and little to no heat. Hot (Hungarian) paprika offers a peppery kick and heat. Smoked paprika, as you may have guessed, is smoky, as it is made from peppers that have been smoked and dried.

Parsley. I always use fresh flat-leaf parsley, also known as Italian parsley, but feel free to use curly-leaf, which is most often associated with decorative garnishes. Don't forget to save the stems! They are just as flavorful as the leaves, and you can use them for making other things, such as broth or–you guessed it–pesto!

Pasta water. Throughout this book, when I share a recipe for preparing pasta or noodles, I call for reserving 1 cup of the pasta water. The reason is simple: The starchy pasta water helps bind and thicken the sauce, and in the case of a buttery or oil-based sauce, the water will emulsify it into a creamy coating. And of course, if your pasta has dried out while waiting to be dressed, a slug of water will rehydrate it quickly.

Salt. I developed these recipes using the dense, granular Morton's variety of kosher salt, as opposed to the lighter, more "flaky" versions you might see elsewhere. If you are using a different brand, your mileage may vary. My suggestion is to start by adding less salt than you think you need, and then season to taste. You can always add more, but the reverse is not so easy!

Scallions. Use both green and white parts, unless otherwise noted. Sometimes, I suggest separating the white from the green, as when one part goes into the recipe and the other is used as garnish.

Sugar. When a recipe calls for "sugar," that means granulated white sugar, the most refined variety. I also sometimes use brown sugar, which is refined or blended with white sugar, and turbinado, which is minimally refined raw cane sugar with large crystals. Any will do in a pinch (ha ha).

A PANTRY PRIMER

Whether you're preparing your pesto in a sprawling suburban home or an apartment kitchenette, the tools and equipment needed for this book can be adapted to fit your needs. The one piece of equipment that is essential to creating your personal pesto is a food processor or blender. Still, there are many other tools you'll find to be your allies in the kitchen. While it isn't essential to have every item on this list, it will provide you with a good base that you can build on.

aluminum foil

baking dishes
Pyrex, ceramic, or oval gratin dishes in a variety of sizes and shapes

baking sheets with a raised rim
small (9 × 13 inches), medium (10 × 15 inches), and large (11 × 17 inches)

blender
8-cup capacity

cast-iron grill pan
any shape

citrus juicer

cookie cutters
various shapes and sizes

Dutch oven
5- to 8-quart capacity

food processor
8- to 12-cup capacity

funnel

garlic press

immersion/stick blender

instant-read thermometer

kitchen scale
digital

kitchen shears

kitchen tongs

knives
chef's, paring, serrated bread, slicing/carving

mandoline

measuring cups
liquid and dry

measuring spoons

meat mallet

melon baller

Microplane zester/grater

mortar and pestle

muffin tins

nonstick skillet with lid
10-inch diameter

nut grinder

oven mitts

panini press

parchment paper

plastic wrap

potato masher

ramekins

rolling pin

rubber spatulas
variety of sizes

salad spinner

saucepans
variety of sizes

silicone baking mats

slotted spoons

soup ladles

spice grinder

spider skimmer

spiralizer

stainless steel skillets
6-, 10-, and 12-inch diameters

vegetable peelers
multiple sizes, plus julienne style

vegetable steamer basket

wax paper

whisks
variety of sizes

wooden skewers
variety of sizes

wooden spoons

BASIC COOKING METHODS

There are a few prepared items that I use in multiple recipes in this book. Everyone has their own way of preparing these ingredients (and many can be found premade at the store), but here I outline my preferred method for each.

Bacon. I use the microwave. It is fast and simple, and cleanup is a breeze! For perfectly crisp bacon (use pork or turkey, cured or uncured, whatever you prefer), place three paper towels on a microwavable plate. Lay the slices of bacon on the paper towels and top with three more paper towels. Microwave the bacon on high, 1 minute per slice. Blot the bacon with paper towels to remove the excess grease. Instead of this method, you can cook bacon on the stovetop or in the oven. Find the method that works best for you.

Broth. A basic vegetable broth is easy to make and so much more flavorful than the store-bought kind. You can save your clean veggie scraps in the freezer until you have enough to make into a batch of broth. One gallon-size zip-top bag full of scraps is usually enough. Or try 1 chopped onion, 2 diced carrots, 2 chopped celery ribs, and 2 minced garlic cloves. Bring 8 cups of water to a boil in a stockpot over medium-high heat. Add the veggies, a handful of chopped fresh herbs (such as parsley, dill, and chives), and salt and pepper to taste. Lower the heat to low and let the broth simmer, uncovered, for 1 hour. Strain the solids from the broth. You can use it right away or store it in an airtight container in the refrigerator for 4 to 5 days or, when cool, transfer the broth to zip-top freezer bags and lay flat in the freezer for up to 3 months.

Hardboiled eggs. Bring a pot of water to a boil over medium-high heat. Carefully place the eggs in the water and add 1 to 2 tablespoons of distilled white vinegar (depending on the number of eggs in your pot). Cover, lower the heat to low, and simmer for 14 minutes. Transfer the eggs to an ice bath and refrigerate for at least 15 minutes. Under cool water, peel and discard the shells. Pat the hardboiled eggs dry. They will keep in the refrigerator for about 3 days.

Rice. People tend to have trouble cooking rice, but it's easy–I promise! It's all about the proportion of water to rice. I've gotten the best results for white and jasmine rice by using one part rice to one and a half parts liquid. The liquid can be water or something more flavorful, such as broth, wine, tea, coconut milk, or a combination of these. Always give your rice a good rinse under cool running water before using it. Let the rice drain in a colander, then transfer it to a large saucepan or stockpot. Add the liquid, cover the pan, and bring the mixture to a boil over medium-high heat. Immediately lower the heat to low and let simmer for 10 minutes, or until all the liquid has been absorbed into the rice. The trick is to keep the lid on–don't be tempted to keep checking on it! Remove the pan from the heat and let the rice sit, still covered, for another 10 minutes. Fluff the rice with a fork and you're ready to go! Always remember that dried rice will triple in size when it is cooked.

Roasted jalapeños. Preheat the oven to 300°F. Cut the jalapeños in half lengthwise and place them, cut side down, on a small baking sheet. Roast for 25 to 30 minutes, until they have slightly shrunken in size, browned, and softened. Remove the jalapeños from the oven and let them cool. To eliminate some of the heat from the jalapeños, don gloves and use a melon baller to remove the seeds and membrane. If you prefer your dish hot and spicy, this step is not necessary.

Toasted nuts. Toasting releases their oils and produces a more fragrant and flavorful nut. Warm a small skillet over low heat and add the nuts (whole preferred), making sure not to crowd them. Watch closely as they toast, shaking the skillet so that the nuts do not stick or burn. When the nuts are lightly golden, transfer them to a plate and cool.

Veggie noodles. I use veggie noodles all the time. Although you can often find premade versions at the grocery store, a spiralizer device makes quick work of creating them at home. Spiralizers are available across all price points in various formats, and most come with attachments for making different types of noodles, such as angel hair, curly ribbons, and thick spaghetti. (You can also use a simple vegetable peeler with a serrated blade.) Some shapes may work better for some vegetables than others.

First, trim your veggie so that there is a flat surface to attach to the pronged dials on the device. If your vegetable is long, like a zucchini or cucumber, try cutting it in quarters before you spiralize so that the noodles you create are manageable on your plate. When using a butternut squash, halve the squash crosswise. Slice off the top and discard. Peel the outer skin. Cut across the squash into 1½-inch-thick medallions before spiralizing. Some vegetables are harder and denser than others and require a little extra muscle to turn the crank. I recommend experimenting with different types of veggies before you try the recipes. My regular spiralized vegetable rotation consists of zucchini, summer squash, beets, butternut squash, cucumbers, radishes (bigger varieties such as daikon, watermelon, purple, and green), onions, bell peppers, large carrots, turnips, rutabaga, and whatever else I find at the farmers market.

The Modern Mother Sauce

(Pesto Basics)

When it comes down to it, most cooking boils down to a few elemental techniques. Put them together in the right order and incorporate some fresh, flavorful ingredients, and a kind of alchemy happens.

One of these culinary building blocks is the concept of the "mother sauce": a base that, as its name suggests, provides the DNA for a wealth of other sauces and dishes. This concept dates back to the 1800s, to the kitchen of Marie-Antoine Carême. This now-legendary chef identified four sauces central to French cuisine. Another chef, Auguste Escoffier, is credited with building upon Carême's work a couple of generations later, when he identified five mother sauces: *béchamel, espagnole, velouté, hollandaise,* and *tomat.*

Ranging from thick and creamy to light and tart, these sauces have served as the building blocks of elegant gastronomy, entering the kitchens of American home cooks through Julia Child's *Mastering the Art of French Cooking.*

Despite this storied past, most of these mother sauces are not used very often in home kitchens today. The modern cook wants recipes that are light, quick, and easy, something that the mother sauces could never claim to be.

Some contemporary chefs have worked to redefine mother sauces, updating them to reflect the modern consciousness of health, seasonality, and economy. Samin Nosrat, author of *Salt, Fat, Acid, Heat,* wrote in the *New York Times* about the "Five Sauces for the Modern Cook," which includes pesto, along with yogurt, pepper, herb—also known as "green sauce"—and tahini. I couldn't agree more.

Basil pesto was first popularized in Liguria, Italy—a beautiful Mediterranean seafaring region where basil has always grown wild and plentiful near the port city of Genoa. The term *pesto* (Italian for "to pound or crush") technically refers to any sauce that was traditionally combined using a mortar and pestle. However, pesto alla Genovese, named after its birthplace, combined six simple, local ingredients—Genovese basil, pungent garlic, creamy pignoli (pine nuts), sharp and nutty Parmigiano Reggiano, salt, and fruity, peppery olive oil—into a delightful paste.

Over time, the originally frugal pesto sauce spread globally, and it assimilated to many other regions, where people started using what was plentiful, local, and in season. Pesto had another culinary moment in the 1980s when *The Silver Palate Cookbook* was introduced to home cooks, and top chefs in New York and California started to think about incorporating regional Italian cooking onto their menus, which shifted pesto from provincial to cosmopolitan. Today, pesto has caught on in a more individual way to include a combination of various herbs, nuts, and cheeses that may be

ORIGINAL MOTHER SAUCES

Béchamel. A white sauce of milk or dairy thickened with a roux (a paste made of butter and flour).

Espagnole. A basic brown sauce made from brown stock, mirepoix (uniformly diced or chopped onions, carrots, and celery), and tomatoes thickened with a roux.

Velouté. A light stock thickened with a roux.

Hollandaise. The only mother sauce not thickened by a roux but rather with an emulsion of egg yolk, melted butter, water, and either lemon juice, white wine, or vinegar; seasoned with salt, black pepper, and cayenne pepper.

Tomat. A red sauce of cooked tomatoes thickened with a roux.

MODERN MOTHER SAUCES

Yogurt. A light, cool, and tangy base of plain yogurt can be enhanced with any number of add-ins to create a sauce to complement your dish.

Pepper. Also known as hot sauce or chili sauce, this blend is made from a spicy pepper base of dried, toasted, roasted, or rehydrated peppers, which provide a flavorful kick to any meal. Let it serve as a starting point, with various add-ins to make your dish anything but ordinary!

Herb. A blend of any herb plus lemon, garlic, vinegar, and oil.

Tahini. A thick sauce made from ground toasted sesame seeds and olive oil.

Pesto. Similar to an herb sauce, with the addition of nuts and cheese.

local or fit your personal preference—and that is where this book comes in.

In general, local, seasonal green sauces are not a new idea; they have long been staples of cooking around the world. The French have the pistou; Argentina has the chimichurri; Spain and Mexico each have their own version of salsa verde; the English have their mint sauce to slather over lamb; and Germany, the grune sosse. Great minds think alike.

I share this history because thinking of pesto as a mother sauce—as a jumping-off point for experimentation or a base layer for culinary development—is the first step in the Hope's Gardens method. Unlike those early mother sauces, this one can come from your backyard, reduce food waste, and deliver healthy, nutritious vegetables into your diet in delicious and surprising ways. Now, I invite you to create your own Modern Mother.

A CLOSER LOOK AT BASIL PESTO INGREDIENTS

Not only is pesto a sensory delight, but if you take a look at the individual ingredients, you will discover it also has many health benefits. Needless to say, I am not a doctor, but I am always interested in treating my family, friends, and myself to nutritious food that tastes great, fuels the body, and leads to a happy and healthy life.

In Classic Basil Pesto (see page 23), the primary herb, **basil**, is rich in beta-carotene, which, after being converted by the body into vitamin A, aids in eye health and immune system function. It is also a wonderful source of flavonoids, which reduce inflammation and have antioxidant and antibacterial properties.

Garlic has been shown to protect the heart by lowering cholesterol levels, stabilizing blood pressure levels, and slowing hardening of the arteries. **Pine nuts** are rich in protein, while **olive oil** is full of heart-healthy monounsaturated fats, which can also lower cholesterol, stabilize blood sugar, and help keep blood clot free. Keeping all these benefits in mind, it is also high in calories.

Parmigiano Reggiano is high in calcium, which builds strong bones, but it also has a relatively high sodium level, which you may want to keep in mind when making your own pesto—in other words, you may not need much additional salt. Lastly, pesto is naturally gluten free!

How to Make Pesto

Remember that in the Hope's Gardens method, pesto is more of an outline than a prescription. Are you allergic to nuts? Vegan? Do you have dairy intolerance? Do you dislike garlic? There is no reason you should miss out on the pleasures of pesto. By using available ingredients thoughtfully and resourcefully, you can generate a version tailored to suit your personal tastes and dietary restrictions.

I encourage you to approach pesto-making with an open mind and a willingness to experiment. This section suggests numerous options—some unconventional—for pesto ingredients. Pesto made from carrot tops, seaweed, or artichoke? Why not!

I've been making pesto and cultivating combinations for more than a decade. I've come to think of pesto as six components (three of which are optional) that you can mix and match as you please. The primary components are plants, nuts/seeds, cheese, garlic, seasoning/acid, and oil. As long as you mix and match in the proportions I outline here, you'll end up with pesto that will hopefully be perfect

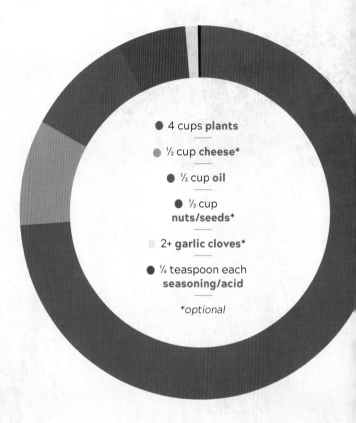

- 4 cups **plants**
- ½ cup **cheese***
- ½ cup **oil**
- ⅓ cup **nuts/seeds***
- 2+ **garlic cloves***
- ¼ teaspoon each **seasoning/acid**

optional

every time. If not, let it serve as a learning experience. Be sure to make notations (good and bad) on your pesto worksheet (see page 199) so the next time you can make the tweaks necessary. Remember that the process of learning is fun and that Rome was not built in a day!

Let's take a closer look at these components so you can really understand how they work together to create something so simple yet so delectable.

PLANTS

Traditionally, this component is basil. I am using the term *plants* quite broadly here—think greens (or reds, purples, oranges, whites), herbs and other leafy things, vegetables, tubers, bulbs, roots, fruits, flowers, pods, you name it. This is the base of your pesto, and it's the ingredient that provides the most pronounced flavor. Start here and build your flavors around it. Don't be afraid to mix and match plants—2 cups peas and 2 cups dill? Give it a whirl! I can't guarantee that every batch will be a winner, but I promise that you will have fun figuring out what plants to use and which to combine. Note that I use 4 cups of chopped plants, unless it has small leaves, such as basil, in which case I use the whole leaves.

artichokes

arugula

asparagus

avocado

basil

beans (all varieties)

beets

beet greens

bok choy

broccoli

broccoli rabe (rapini)

brussels sprouts

cabbage

carrot tops

carrots

cauliflower

celery

celery root (celeriac)

chard

chervil

cilantro

collards

corn

dill

edamame

eggplant

escarole

fennel

figs

garlic scapes

jalapeño

kale

leeks

mint

mustard greens

olives

onions

parsley

parsnips

peas (all varieties)

peppers (all varieties)

radicchio

radishes

ramps

rutabaga greens

seaweed

shiso

sorrel

spinach

squash (all varieties)

sun-dried tomatoes

tomatillos

tomatoes (all varieties)

turnip greens

turnips

watercress

zucchini

CHEESE / CHEESE SUBSTITUTES
(OPTIONAL)

Cheese contributes a degree of saltiness and a textural bite to your pesto. Parmigiano Reggiano is traditionally used, but you can use almost any medium to hard cheese you wish. I grate or shred my cheese before measuring. I find that soft cheeses don't work as well when making pesto. I prefer to add them later to create a creamy and delicious dressing, topping, or dip. (You will find many recipes throughout this book for these.) If you don't eat dairy, nutritional yeast, vegan cheese, or even tahini are good stand-ins for cheese.

Asiago	Gouda (aged)	miso	Pecorino Romano
cheddar (aged)	Grana Padano	nutritional yeast	ricotta salata
Cotija	Gruyère	parmesan	tahini
feta	Manchego	Parmigiano Reggiano	vegan cheese (any variety)

OIL

I can't imagine a traditional basil pesto without the glorious fruity and buttery flavors of olive oil (extra virgin is best). Oil is the binder that holds all the pesto ingredients together, allowing it to become a uniform sauce. Although you can't go wrong with olive oil, try experimenting with different oils to see what kind of subtle flavor they can bring to the party. If you want your seasonings to be the star of the show, you may consider a mild or neutral oil, such as canola. If you're going for a global flavor profile, try an oil that is commonly used in the region. No matter which one you use, always taste the oil you are using to make sure it is bright and flavorful. You will know right away if it is bad or rancid, which can happen if the oil is improperly stored, experiences temperature swings, or is just plain old.

avocado	extra virgin olive	peanut	walnut
canola	grapeseed	safflower	
coconut	hazelnut	sesame	
corn	olive	sunflower	

NUTS / SEEDS (OPTIONAL)

The traditional nut used in pesto is buttery-flavored pine nuts. Their price can be volatile. A few years back there was a global shortage due to adverse weather conditions, which reduced supply and increased prices. You do not need to be restricted to this or any other nut—almost any will do. Nuts act to thicken the pesto and create a creamy consistency. If nuts aren't a part of your diet, seeds can serve the same purpose. You'll want to make sure your nuts are not stale or rancid, as this will affect your pesto. To kick the flavor up a notch, consider toasting your nuts (see my method on page 9). If you are using a small nut or seed, measure them whole according to the pesto template, but if you are using a larger nut or seed, such as almonds, walnuts, or pepitas, chop them in a nut grinder before measuring. It makes it easier to measure out and blend into the mixture. I list nuts and seeds as optional because if you have an allergy or do not like them, you can still enjoy the pleasures of pesto. Try adding a bit more cheese to compensate for the absence of nuts or seeds.

almonds	flax seeds	pecans	sesame seeds
cashews	hazelnuts	pine nuts (pignoli)	sunflower seeds
chestnuts	macadamia nuts	pistachios	walnuts
chia seeds	peanuts	pumpkin seeds (pepitas)	

GARLIC (OPTIONAL)

I love garlic! But, I understand it's not to everyone's liking. In fact, I had a customer in Atlanta who loved garlic but his girlfriend did not. He requested I make special batches of pesto without garlic so he could prepare meals for the two of them. We would rendezvous in the Whole Foods parking lot so I could make the drop-off. Garlic provides a pungent, spicy flavor to pesto. Use as much or as little as you like—I have been known to use up to six cloves in a small batch. If you're looking for a gentler flavor, try roasting the garlic before adding it to your pesto. Slice off the top of a whole head, drizzle on some olive oil, add a pinch of salt, wrap in aluminum foil, and roast in a 400°F oven for about 30 minutes. This will mellow the garlic flavor and release its sugars, providing a bit of sweetness.

SEASONING / ACID

This is where you can really make your pesto shine. I recommend you always start with about ¼ teaspoon each of salt and pepper. Next, try mixing things up with your seasonings—almost any spice, condiment, or acid can add extra flavor, aroma, brightness, or color to your pesto. Start with one or two additional seasonings, which could include spices, citrus zest and juice, or just about anything listed below. Make sure to note what and how much you use on your worksheet, so you can replicate it or adjust it as needed. You are in charge of how salty, sweet, bold, or delicate you'd like your pesto to be. Fun fact: You are getting all this flavor without any fat! If you aren't sure where to start, consider tried-and-true flavor combinations from around the world (see page 21). For example, an Indian-inspired pesto might include coriander, cumin, and cinnamon, while an Asian-inspired pesto might use ginger, lime zest and juice, and curry powder.

allspice	curry powder	nutmeg	salt
capers	dill weed	orange	scallions
caraway	fennel seeds (anise)	oregano	shallots
cardamom		paprika (any variety)	star anise
cayenne	five-spice powder		sugar
celery seeds	ginger	peppercorns (any variety)	tarragon
chili powder	ginseng		thyme
chives	herbes de Provence	poppy seeds	turmeric
cinnamon	lemon	red pepper flakes	wasabi
cloves	lime	rosemary	yuzu
coriander	marjoram	saffron	za'atar
cumin	mustard seeds	sage	

PUTTING IT ALL TOGETHER

Once you've chosen your ingredients, putting them all together is easy. I prefer to use a food processor, but you can also use a blender or mortar and pestle, or put some elbow grease into it with a fork or whisk. Wash and dry your plants and herbs. Place all your ingredients, except the oil, in the bowl of your food processor. Pulse a few times to combine them. Then, slowly add the oil through the feed tube while pulsing for several seconds, until the mixture has a paste-like consistency. Use a rubber spatula to scrape down the sides of the bowl, then pulse a few more times. If you prefer a smoother pesto, add more oil, a few drops at a time, until you achieve the consistency you are looking for.

Preserving Your Pesto and Using Up Leftovers

Maybe you're a meal-prepper. Maybe you're planning a big party and are looking to work ahead. Or maybe you're just looking for the best way to deal with leftover pesto. Whatever your reason, having a sure-fire way of preserving and using up remnants is resourceful and timesaving.

There are a couple of things to understand about pesto. First, it will last in an airtight container in the refrigerator for up to five days. Keep in mind that many herbs and vegetables have a high moisture content, which can lead to spoilage after a few days, so it's best to use your pesto fast and make more frequently. Second, pesto is highly susceptible to oxidation, an unappetizing change in color due to exposure to the air. While the browning won't kill you, it's not very appealing. Here are a few tried-and-true techniques for preserving and using up your homemade treasures.

Freeze it. There are two convenient ways I have found to do this: in an ice cube tray and in a freezer bag. For the ice cube tray method, simply add pesto to each compartment and pop it in the freezer. Once the pesto cubes are frozen (it will normally take 6 to 8 hours; I just leave mine overnight), transfer them to a freezer bag or plastic container and use as needed. (See the Gazpacho Shooters recipe on page 114 for inspiration.) Look for easy-release ice cube trays. Depending on the size of your tray, each cube will be between 1/4 teaspoon (for a mini tray) and 2 tablespoons (for a standard tray), which is great when measuring for recipes. The pesto cubes will keep for about 6 months–if they last that long! For the freezer bag method, pour the pesto into a zip-top freezer bag, then squeeze out as much air as possible before sealing. Lay the bag flat to save space in your freezer. Once the pesto is frozen, you can snap

off as much as you want whenever you need it. When you freeze pesto, you generally don't have to worry about defrosting it before popping it into something like a soup or stew, as within moments it will incorporate into whatever you have on the stove. Much like the freezer bag method, if you have a food vacuum sealer or FoodSaver machine at home, follow the product instructions and pop your pesto in the freezer.

Refrigerate it. If you know you'll be using your pesto within a few days, you can keep it in the fridge. To prevent browning, top the pesto with a thin layer of olive oil. This will essentially create a barrier between the pesto and the air. When ready to use, mix the oil into the pesto and proceed with your recipe.

Dress it up. If a little pesto remains in your jar, add a bit of balsamic or wine vinegar and shake it in the jar. Now you have a delicious dressing or vinaigrette and have not wasted a bit of your precious pesto.

Mix it up. To create a pesto-infused oil to drizzle over soups, salads, or whatever else strikes your fancy, combine leftover pesto with a buttery, sweet olive oil. Alternatively, try neutral-tasting oils that are less assertive, such as grapeseed, canola, or safflower. Start with whatever pesto remains in the jar and add 1/2 cup oil. Give it a shake, and if it tastes good, then you are set to drizzle away. What differentiates this from salad dressing or vinaigrette is the lack of acid (vinegar or citrus), which balances and brightens the flavor. Refrigerate your pesto-infused oil as soon as possible to avoid spoilage.

Share it. A big batch of pesto makes a wonderful surprise for friends and family! Bring some to your next dinner party to enjoy with some crusty bread, or wrap it up with some wine and cheese for a lovely holiday gift. When Hope's Gardens was selling at the holiday farmers market, we had a gift pack of one jar each of Classic Basil Pesto (page 23), Sun-Dried Tomato Pesto (page 30), and Roasted Jalapeño–Cilantro Pesto (page 30). Not only were the colors perfect for the holidays, but the flavors were mouth watering and perfect for preparing Silky Pesto Goat Cheese Terrine (see page 96).

Basic Pesto Recipes

WITHIN THIS SECTION ARE tried-and-true recipes that will become staples in your daily arsenal. I keep these prepared and ready to use on sandwiches, paninis, and wraps that would otherwise be missing a bit of flavor. There will be times when you want your pesto fix but don't feel like making any of the recipes in this book. That's okay. Just pull out a prepared basic pesto and add it to whatever you have going on.

A GUIDE TO GLOBAL FLAVOR PROFILES

Some of my recipes include an international spin on a familiar (generally American) classic. In these cases, I find it's best to pair the dish with a pesto that shares a flavor profile from the same family. For example, if you're making Chicken Pesto Fried Rice (see page 154), a Thai-inspired, cilantro-and-peanut pesto will complement the dish much better than an Italian sun-dried tomato pesto.

If you've never tried your hand at preparing a Chinese, Cajun, Indian, or Mediterranean dish, don't sweat. Here are a few suggestions for effective flavor combinations you can use as inspiration to create flavors from around the world.

Cajun. Celery, garlic, green bell peppers, onions, parsley, paprika, shallots

Chinese. Chiles, chives, cilantro, five-spice powder, garlic, ginger, scallions, shallots, star anise

French. Bay leaves, carrots, celery, herbes de Provence, onions, parsley, thyme

Indian. Cardamom, chiles, cloves, cumin, curry powder, garam masala (a blend of bay leaf, cardamom, cinnamon, cloves, coriander, cumin, peppercorns, and nutmeg), garlic, ginger, onions, tomatoes, turmeric

Italian. Bay leaves, carrots, celery, fennel, garlic, onions, parsley, sage

Latin American. Bay leaves, bell peppers, chiles, cilantro, coriander, cumin, garlic, onions, paprika, tomatoes

Middle Eastern. Cinnamon, garlic, ginger, onions, raisins, saffron, scallions, tomatoes, turmeric

Thai. Cashews, chiles, cilantro, galangal (a relative of ginger, with a citrusy flavor), garlic, lemongrass, makrut limes (a small bumpy-rind lime with a strong acidic taste), peanuts, shallots, Thai basil

Classic Basil Pesto

MAKES ABOUT 1 CUP
🕐 **READY IN 10 MINUTES**

4 cups basil leaves
⅓ cup pine nuts
½ cup grated
    Parmigiano
    Reggiano
6 garlic cloves, or
    to taste
¼ teaspoon salt
¼ teaspoon pepper
½ cup extra virgin
    olive oil

There is no substitute for picking the basil fresh off the plant and making pesto within minutes. If you have home-grown basil of your own, I think you'll feel the same way! But if you don't have access to a garden, don't worry. Basil from the grocery store will do just fine.

Combine all the ingredients except the olive oil in a food processor. Pulse for several seconds, until the mixture turns into a paste. Slowly add the olive oil through the feed tube while pulsing, then pulse for about 10 seconds. Scrape down the sides and pulse once or twice more. If you prefer a smoother, looser consistency, add a little more olive oil and continue pulsing. When the pesto is to your liking, use immediately or transfer it to a jar, top with a thin layer of olive oil, cover, and refrigerate until ready to use.

A Few of Hope's Gardens Favorites

We started our business with Classic Basil Pesto, but as customers embraced this flavor, our business grew—and our regulars wanted new flavors. It pays to experiment! I created the following combinations, which have also become our customers' favorites. Feel free to use these as a starting point to create your own combinations.

ROASTED JALAPEÑO-CILANTRO

RECIPE ON PAGE 30

cilantro, jalapeños

pine nuts

Parmigiano Reggiano

garlic

salt and pepper

olive oil

SUN-DRIED TOMATO

RECIPE ON PAGE 30

sun-dried tomatoes

Parmigiano Reggiano

capers, chives, turbinado sugar, salt and pepper

olive oil

KALE

RECIPE ON PAGE 31

kale

almonds

Parmigiano Reggiano

garlic

lemon juice and zest, shallots, salt and pepper

olive oil

ARUGULA

arugula

pistachios

Parmigiano Reggiano

garlic

lemon juice, salt and pepper

olive oil

FENNEL

fennel, spinach, sweet onion

garlic

thyme, salt and pepper

olive oil

MINT

RECIPE ON PAGE 31

green peas, mint, parsley

almonds

garlic

lemon juice, scallions,
salt and pepper

olive oil

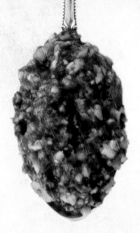

DILL

dill

almonds

Parmigiano Reggiano

garlic

salt and pepper

olive oil

PARSLEY

parsley

pecans

Parmigiano Reggiano

garlic

salt and pepper

olive oil

LEMON

lemons

almonds

garlic

salt and pepper

olive oil

SPINACH

spinach

candied pecans

Parmigiano Reggiano

garlic

salt and pepper

olive oil

OLIVE

RECIPE ON PAGE 32

green olives stuffed with
sweet peppers, Kalamata
olives, sun-dried tomatoes

garlic

anchovies, capers, herbes
de Provence, pepper

olive oil

Thai-Inspired Pesto Vinaigrette

MAKES ABOUT 1½ CUPS

⏱ READY IN 10 MINUTES

This simple vinaigrette is a wonderful addition to the Spicy Thai-Inspired Noodle recipe on page 55. You may find yourself also pouring it over a bowl of jasmine rice or a quick vegetable stir-fry.

1 cup Thai-inspired pesto (think cilantro, Thai basil, peanuts, cashews)
½ cup rice wine vinegar
2½ tablespoons lime juice
2 teaspoons toasted sesame oil

Combine all the ingredients in a lidded jar. Shake well. Serve immediately or store in the refrigerator for up to 2 weeks.

VINAIGRETTE VERSUS DRESSING

A vinaigrette is a dressing, but a dressing is not a vinaigrette. Why? Vinaigrettes are a combination of oil and an acid, such as citrus or vinegar. The traditional balance is two to three parts oil to one part acid. I like to play around with this ratio, and when you add pesto—which typically already has ½ cup oil—you will see why my classic vinaigrette uses less oil. Dressing is a little more involved. It can have a base of mayonnaise, buttermilk, avocado, yogurt, or a vinaigrette. Additional ingredients, such as garlic, mustard, or other condiments, act to bind these elements together and create a flavorful dressing. Many of the binding ingredients are inherent in the pesto.

Classic Pesto Vinaigrette

MAKES ABOUT 3 CUPS

⏱ READY IN 10 MINUTES

You will probably find yourself using this vinaigrette on a variety of greens and grain salads as well as a flavorful marinade for roasting vegetables. That is why I recommend you make a big batch! Feel free to halve the recipe if you don't cook a lot. We use this in our Caprese Salad recipe on page 134.

1 cup pesto
Juice of 2 lemons
1 cup olive oil
1 cup white or red wine vinegar
Salt and pepper, to taste

Combine all the ingredients in a lidded jar. Shake well. Serve immediately or store in the refrigerator for up to 2 weeks.

Tangy Pesto Vinaigrette

MAKES ABOUT 1½ CUPS

⏱ READY IN 10 MINUTES

The difference between this dressing and the Classic Pesto Vinaigrette is that we up the acid a bit, creating a sharp, tangy vinaigrette. There's no need for additional olive oil, as there is already some in the pesto. I recommend you use this dressing in our "One and Done" Chicken and Veggie Plate recipe (see page 158), but it also works great on a shaved fennel salad or a brussels sprouts slaw.

1 cup pesto
Juice of 2 lemons
6 tablespoons white wine vinegar
Salt and pepper, to taste

Combine all the ingredients in a lidded jar. Shake well. Serve immediately or store in the refrigerator for up to 2 weeks.

Pesto Mayo

MAKES 1 CUP
○ READY IN 5 MINUTES

This is a classic recipe that no kitchen should be without. It makes every sandwich taste better. The added lemon juice will keep your mayo fresh and the flavor and color bright.

½ cup pesto
½ cup mayonnaise
1 teaspoon lemon juice

Combine all the ingredients in a lidded jar. Mix well. Serve immediately or store in the refrigerator for up to 1 month.

Spicy Pesto Aioli

MAKES ABOUT 1½ CUPS
○ READY IN 10 MINUTES

Build on a simple aioli with the spicy goodness of mustard and additional garlic, along with pesto to ramp up the flavor. It's the perfect complement to Grilled Eggplant Roll-Ups (see page 100) or Sizzling Chicken Pesto Fajitas (page 157), but I also love it on a simple grilled cheese panini or shrimp taco.

½ cup pesto
½ cup mayonnaise
4 garlic cloves, minced
4 teaspoons spicy mustard
2 tablespoons olive oil
2 tablespoons lemon juice

Combine all the ingredients in a lidded jar. Mix well. Serve immediately or store in the refrigerator for up to 1 month.

Buttermilk Pesto Dressing

MAKES ABOUT 1 CUP
○ READY IN 10 MINUTES

I have many memories of moist buttermilk biscuits from my days in Atlanta, and I created this tangy dressing with them in mind. Use it on our Summer Greens salad (see page 132) or add it to mashed potatoes. If you do not have buttermilk, add 1 tablespoon lemon juice to 1 cup milk. Stir and wait a few minutes, until it has thickened slightly. That's it! Use any leftover buttermilk in pancakes, muffins, or cakes.

½ cup buttermilk
½ cup pesto
2 tablespoons white wine vinegar
Salt and pepper, to taste

Combine all the ingredients in a lidded jar. Shake well. Serve immediately or store in the refrigerator for up to 1 week.

Kale Pesto Dressing

MAKES ABOUT 1½ CUPS
○ READY IN 10 MINUTES

Kale often gets a bad rap, but I don't buy into that. I eat kale several times a week, and I always have a jar of kale pesto ready to go in the refrigerator, especially for this dressing recipe. I toss it onto a kale Caesar salad and top it with shaved parmesan. Or try preparing an avocado and grain salad with this dressing. You will also find it used on our Winter Greens salad recipe (page 132).

½ cup Kale Pesto (page 31)
½ cup white wine vinegar
½ cup olive oil
4 teaspoons lemon juice
Salt and pepper, to taste

Combine all the ingredients in a lidded jar. Shake well. Serve immediately or store in the refrigerator for up to 2 weeks.

Compound Pesto Butter

MAKES 1 STICK

⏱ READY IN 10 MINUTES

1 stick butter, at room
temperature
½ cup pesto

These pesto butters are a lifesaver. Have four or five differ-ent flavor combinations in your freezer or refrigerator at any given time, and if you love to entertain, grab a few of your favorite flavors, bring to room temperature, and get the party started. You can use them for everything from glazing grilled fish, beef, or chicken to adding more flavor to a toasted bagel or, of course, a simple buttered pasta dish. For another way to use these butters, see the "Always Make Extra" Potatoes recipe on page 139.

Combine the butter and pesto in a small bowl. Lay a 16-inch-long sheet of plastic wrap on a clean work surface. Transfer the pesto-flavored butter to the center of the plastic wrap. Using the plastic, form it into an approximately 2½ × 8-inch log (similar to slice-and-bake cookie dough). Wrap tightly in the plastic wrap, twisting the ends like a wrapped hard candy, and store in the refrigerator for up to 1 month or in the freezer for up to 4 months.

SERVING SUGGESTIONS FOR A COCKTAIL PARTY: Cut a variety of breads, and place them in a large basket. Gather smaller bowls to put out various cheeses, jams, sliced hardboiled eggs, and compound pesto butter. Other options would be watermelon radish slices, cucumber slices, figs, roasted peppers, apple and peach slices, and mixed nuts.

Roasted Jalapeño-Cilantro Pesto

MAKES ABOUT 1 CUP
READY IN 10 MINUTES

This special pesto flavor was a favorite when we were regulars at the farmers markets. The sweetness of the roasted jalapeños paired with the cilantro's coolness creates a unique flavor everyone must experience! It can be used in recipes throughout this book, such as the Silky Pesto Goat Cheese Terrine (page 96), Naan Pizza with Fig and Jalapeño Pesto (page 66), Spicy Thai-Inspired Noodles (see page 55), and Spicy Jalapeño Guacamole (page 102).

3 jalapeños, roasted (see method on
    page 6)
2 cups cilantro
⅓ cup pine nuts
½ cup grated Parmigiano Reggiano
3 garlic cloves
¼ teaspoon salt
¼ teaspoon pepper
½ cup olive oil

Combine all the ingredients except the olive oil in a food processor. Pulse for several seconds, until the mixture turns into a paste. Slowly add the olive oil through the feed tube while pulsing, then pulse for about 10 seconds. Scrape down the sides and pulse once or twice more. If you prefer a smoother, looser consistency, add a little more olive oil and continue pulsing. When the pesto is to your liking, use immediately or transfer it to a jar, top with a thin layer of olive oil, cover, and refrigerate for up to 1 week. The roasted jalapeños have a high water content and thus a shorter shelf life, so make sure to taste first before serving.

Sun-Dried Tomato Pesto

MAKES ABOUT 1½ CUPS
READY IN 10 MINUTES

This is a steadfast favorite in our kitchen, and good to have around to serve those who are garlic averse. Both savory and sweet, thanks to the addition of turbinado sugar, it will hold up well when paired with a shrimp dish or a creamy goat cheese appetizer. I use it as the middle layer of our Silky Pesto Goat Cheese Terrine (see page 96).

1 cup soaked and drained sun-dried
    tomatoes
1 teaspoon capers
2 tablespoons Parmigiano Reggiano
1 tablespoon minced chives
⅛ teaspoon turbinado sugar
⅛ teaspoon salt
⅛ teaspoon pepper
½ cup olive oil

Combine all the ingredients except the olive oil in a food processor. Pulse for several seconds, until the mixture turns into a paste. Slowly add the olive oil through the feed tube while pulsing, then pulse for about 10 seconds. Scrape down the sides and pulse once or twice more. If you prefer a smoother, looser consistency, add a little more olive oil and continue pulsing. When the pesto is to your liking, transfer it to a jar, use immediately or top with a layer of olive oil, cover, and refrigerate until ready to use.

Mint Pesto

MAKES ABOUT 1 CUP
⊘ READY IN 10 MINUTES

This is a lovely spring pesto that pairs well with a lamb dish (such as the Mint Pesto Lamb Kebabs on page 192), a springtime minestrone soup (see our Pesto Minestrone for All Seasons on page 116), or a fresh pea salad. You could also use it any time of year to remind you of the fresh flavors of spring.

1 cup mint
½ cup parsley
¼ cup frozen green peas
2 tablespoons almonds, toasted (see method on page 9)
1 garlic clove
2 tablespoons sliced scallions
¼ teaspoon lemon juice
⅛ teaspoon salt
⅛ teaspoon pepper
⅓ cup olive oil

Combine all the ingredients except the olive oil in a food processor. Pulse for several seconds, until the mixture turns into a paste. Slowly add the olive oil through the feed tube while pulsing, then pulse for about 10 seconds. Scrape down the sides and pulse once or twice more. If you prefer a smoother, looser consistency, add a little more olive oil and continue pulsing. When the pesto is to your liking, use immediately or transfer it to a jar, top with a layer of olive oil, cover, and refrigerate until ready to use.

Kale Pesto

MAKES 1 CUP
⊘ READY IN 10 MINUTES

This is another workhorse in our kitchen. Several recipes throughout the book highlight this favorite: Ode to ABC Pizza (page 65), Kale Pesto and Shiitake Mushroom Crostini (page 91), Butternut Squash Spaghetti (page 143), Winter Greens salad (page 132), and wintertime Pesto Minestrone for All Seasons (page 116).

3 cups kale (either curly or Lacinato)
¼ cup almonds, toasted (see method on page 9)
⅓ cup Parmigiano Reggiano
2-3 garlic cloves
1 tablespoon sliced shallot
⅛ teaspoon grated lemon zest
¾ teaspoon lemon juice
⅛ teaspoon salt
⅛ teaspoon pepper
⅓ cup olive oil

Combine all the ingredients except the olive oil in a food processor. Pulse for several seconds, until the mixture turns into a paste. Slowly add the olive oil through the feed tube while pulsing, then pulse for about 10 seconds. Scrape down the sides and pulse once or twice more. If you prefer a smoother, looser consistency, add a little more olive oil and continue pulsing. When the pesto is to your liking, use immediately or transfer it to a jar, top with a layer of olive oil, cover, and refrigerate until ready to use.

Olive Pesto

MAKES ABOUT 2 CUPS
⏱ READY IN 10 MINUTES

Is there really any difference between pesto and tapenade? Not in my book. This tapenade-inspired pesto makes entertaining easy! Set it out with a bowl of tortilla chips, call a few friends over, and pour a cold beer–what could be better! The salty, savory taste also pairs well with our Cedar-Wrapped Halibut (page 168), or use it on a melted Gruyère cheese sandwich.

1 cup Kalamata olives
1 cup green olives stuffed with sweet peppers
½ cup soaked and drained sun-dried tomatoes
2 tablespoons drained capers
2 anchovy fillets
2 garlic cloves
½ teaspoon pepper
¼ teaspoon herbes de Provence
¼ cup olive oil

Combine all the ingredients except the olive oil in a food processor. Pulse for several seconds, until the mixture turns into a paste. Slowly add the olive oil through the feed tube while pulsing, then pulse for about 10 seconds. Scrape down the sides and pulse once or twice more. If you prefer a smoother, looser consistency, add a little more olive oil and continue pulsing. When the pesto is to your liking, use immediately or transfer it to a jar, top with a layer of olive oil, cover, and refrigerate until ready to use.

Green Goddess Pesto

MAKES ABOUT 1 CUP
⏱ READY IN 10 MINUTES

Green goddess originated as a vibrant dressing for romaine lettuce. It was created as a tribute to the actor George Arliss, who in 1923 performed in a play called *The Green Goddess*. Being green, it fits perfectly into becoming pesto. The combination of anchovies, garlic, herbs, cheese, and creamy pistachio nuts is divine on everything. Try it on a Green Goddess Pesto Grilled Cheese (page 87).

2 cups basil
2 cups parsley
½ cup chives
1 tablespoon tarragon
⅓ cup pistachios
½ cup grated Parmigiano Reggiano
2 garlic cloves
2 anchovy fillets
¼ teaspoon salt
¼ teaspoon pepper
½ cup olive oil

Combine all the ingredients except the olive oil in a food processor. Pulse for several seconds, until the mixture turns into a paste. Slowly add the olive oil through the feed tube while pulsing, then pulse for about 10 seconds. Scrape down the sides and pulse once or twice more. If you prefer a smoother, looser consistency, add a little more olive oil and continue pulsing. When the pesto is to your liking, use immediately or transfer it to a jar, top with a layer of olive oil, cover, and refrigerate until ready to use.

Growing Basil at Home

DAVE LENNOX

You know by now that basil is a central ingredient in traditional pesto—but did you know that it is remarkably easy to grow and harvest? Basil is a member of the mint family. Here's a fun fact that I picked up in college biology class: All species of mint have square stems! Like other types of mint, basil is a prolific herb that can be harvested many times during its growing season before it finally goes to flower and seed. Basil is a warm-weather annual that thrives when planted in sunny locations receiving 6 to 8 hours of direct sunlight a day. However, these plants do not tolerate frost, or temperatures below freezing, so be sure to wait until the risk of the last winter frost has passed before outdoor planting. The outdoor growing season comes to an end with the first winter freeze.

There are more than thirty varieties of basil, but I prefer either sweet basil or Genovese basil (the kind used in the original pesto alla Genovese), as I find their fragrance and taste are the best for making pesto. Basil seeds can be purchased at most nurseries or garden stores. I am partial to Johnny's Selected Seeds, a company based in Maine—you can view their inventory and order on-line. However, if you are new to garden-ing, it may be easier to grow your basil from cuttings, or simply buy starter plants from the nursery. The former is a great option if you already have plants that you want to keep going or multiply or if you have a friend who is willing to share with you.

The following few pages provide in-structions for planting basil under four different sets of circumstances. Note that I prefer using a seed starter mix when starting with seeds. This light, airy blend of sphagnum moss, perlite, and other soil-like materials is "fluffy," which allows the seeds to germinate and grow in both directions (roots grow down and stems grow up) without having to fight their way through tradi-tional soil.

Starting from Seed Indoors

If you have a greenhouse or a south-facing window with a sill that receives a lot of direct sunlight, you can start your basil plants from seed indoors. (Using a grow light is another indoor option if none of the above conditions are available.) Plan to get started 4 to 6 weeks before the last frost is expected. If you are planning to transplant your seedlings outdoors, the starter container can be as small as the 2-inch square cells found in seed-starting trays, or larger, such as a plastic drinking cup with holes poked in the bottom for drainage. If you are not planning to transplant the seedlings, your original pot can be any size you want, as long as it's at least 6 inches wide and 6 inches deep and there are drainage holes.

Purchase a bag of seed starter soil mix from your local nursery or home improvement store. This mix is typically moist right out of the bag. If not, add a small amount of water and mix the soil together until you can form a clump by squeezing some soil mix in your hand. However, it shouldn't be so moist so that it turns to mud. Fill your pot or seed starter cells almost to the top. Plant three to five seeds in each cell (more if you are using a larger pot), then cover these seeds with a thin layer of moist seed starter mix. This creates a soil surface under which your seeds can grow undisturbed without being blown or washed away when watering. Using a spray bottle or other misting device, gently mist the top of the soil until the top inch or so is saturated with water. If you are using a store-bought seed-starter tray, it may come with a clear plastic lid. If you cover the seed-starting tray with the lid, you may not need to water the seeds again until they germinate. If you are planting in cups or other containers without a lid, mist daily. Your seeds should germinate within 3 to 7 days, depending on your conditions.

Once germinated, water your seedlings two or three times each week, or when the top layer of soil becomes dry. You can continue to mist the plants from the top, or you can place the tray, cup, or container in a bowl of standing water to moisten from below. This latter option is preferred, as it provides the roots with moisture without the risk of knocking the young plants over with too much water from above.

Starting from Cuttings Indoors (Propagation)

This method is ideal if you already have healthy basil plants on hand. If done properly, stems cut from an existing plant will grow roots that form the basis for a new plant, all without harming the original plant.

Start with a healthy, thriving basil plant that is growing either indoors or outside. We will call this the "donor" plant. You need to look for relatively new growth on the donor plant, as propagation does not occur with old woody growth. Cut a 3- to 4-inch length of stem from the donor plant, making the cut right above a two-leaf node. Gently remove all lower leaves

Stems cut from an existing basil plant will grow roots that form the basis for a new plant, all without harming the original plant.

Basil seedlings in the greenhouse awaiting transplant to the garden.

from the freshly cut stem, leaving only the top two leaves on the stem.

Fill a clear glass with fresh water, and place the freshly cut stem in the glass so that the two top leaves are dry, resting above the water, and the stem is submerged. Using clear glass allows you to watch the new roots grow. Replace the water with fresh water every couple of days. After about a week, small roots will begin to emerge from the bottom of the stem. Continue this process for a total of 3 to 4 weeks. By that time, you'll have substantial root growth, and your cutting will be ready to be planted in soil. If you plan to grow the plant indoors, you can transplant to a larger pot—almost any size will do. If planting outdoors, follow the directions under "Buying a Small Starter Plant and Planting It Outdoors."

Dave transplanting basil with irrigation.

Planting from Seed Outside

This approach shares some of the qualities of starting from seeds indoors, except you must make use of the soil in your garden as the base rather than seed starter mix. To ensure that the soil is loose enough to allow the seeds to germinate, till the garden bed. A mechanical tiller is ideal. (We were fortunate enough to "inherit" a large Troy-Bilt tiller when we bought the house. It was a powerful machine that could turn even the most compact soil into a light, fluffy, growing medium.) Till the soil as deep as you can. If you do not have a mechanical tiller, a shovel and some elbow grease will suffice.

Dig and turn the soil as deep as you can in parallel rows 18 inches apart and approximately as wide as the shovelhead. If you are using a shovel, go back and further loosen up the dirt in each row by turning the shovelhead 90 degrees so it is parallel to the row itself, then chopping and turning the soil to get rid of any clumps. Once your rows have been created, take a thin stick and draw a straight line down the middle of each row (I use a 3-foot length of ½-inch-wide wood doweling, which allows me to do this without bending over). Your goal is to create a furrow that is approximately ¼ inch deep and that runs the entire length of each row you just created. Place three to five seeds together every 12 inches along the entire length of each row. (Note that nurseries and online seed stores sell a handy device that meters out small seeds when planting like this—well worth the $7.)

Finally, come back with a bag of seed starter mix. Take a handful, and rubbing your hands together, gently cover the seeds with a light dusting about ¼ inch thick. This keeps the seeds from blowing or washing away while creating a very light surface that the seeds can easily pop up through as they germinate. Water each row using the mist setting on a garden hose nozzle. The seeds should germinate within 7 to 10 days, and you are off to the races.

Buying a Small Starter Plant and Planting It Outdoors

No doubt, this is the easiest way to get started. However, depending on how much basil you plan to grow, it can quickly become expensive. If you have a mechanical tiller, go ahead and till your entire garden bed. Nothing looks better than a freshly tilled bed with no plants in it! If you do not have a mechanical tiller, all you need to do is dig one hole for each plant you plan to transplant. Try to dig each hole 1 foot deep and 1 foot across. Then, fill the hole loosely with the soil you just removed until the hole is as deep as the soil root ball on your store-bought basil plant. Gently remove the plant from its container and place it in the fresh hole. Gently fill in dirt around the roots up to the bottom of the stem. Once you have finished planting all the basil plants, give them some water. Given the maturity of these plants, you do not have to mist the rows but can apply a light spray.

This method works for planting all types of basil, including seedlings you started indoors.

Once your basil plants are in the ground, they are relatively low maintenance. You will need to water every 3 to 4 days, unless of course it has rained during that time. If it is possible to water only the lower parts of the plants or the soil at the base, that is ideal and will minimize the chance of disease or powdery mildew.

Basil plants are prolific growers and can be harvested frequently. You can begin harvesting when your plants are 6 to 8 inches tall. In a manner similar to what is described on page 34 for propagation, you should cut the stems right above a two-leaf node. This will provide you with all of the leaves on the freshly cut stem and encourage the plant to grow more stems and leaves, thereby becoming bushier. You can harvest regularly throughout the growing season. As fall approaches, the sun starts traveling lower in the sky and the temperatures begin to fall; your basil plants will channel their energy from growing to reproducing. Flowers will begin to form on the tips of some stems, and eventually seeds will develop inside the flowers. When this happens, the basil leaves become less aromatic and the taste begins to turn somewhat bitter. You can forestall the inevitable by pinching off the flowers as they begin to form. This allows you to continue harvesting for another few weeks before the plant, in its drive to perpetuate, will ultimately flower and turn to seed.

If you allow the plants to brown out at the end of the season, you can reclaim the seeds from the dying flowers and use them to start your basil garden next spring.

If your indoor growing conditions will permit, you can propagate some cuttings from your outdoor plants and start the process all over again for basil through the winter. However, a grow light is most likely required for this. ✎

Eggs and Toasts

Eggs and toast aren't just for breakfast, and pesto isn't just for dinner. These recipes illustrate that a personalized pesto can liven up easy egg- or toast-based meals for any time of day.

Green Eggs and Ham in a Shell

MAKES 12 SERVINGS FOR PASTRY SHELLS OR 24 SERVINGS FOR PASTRY CUPS
◷ READY IN 75 MINUTES

2 (6-count) packages frozen puff
    pastry shells or 1 (24-count)
    package frozen puff pastry cups,
    thawed
3 eggs
¼ cup crème fraîche or sour cream
2 cups chopped vegetables,
    greens, and/or mixed herbs
¼ cup pesto
½ cup chopped cooked bacon
    (see method on page 8)
1 cup shredded or grated cheese,
    such as Gruyère or parmesan
Salt and pepper, to taste

Dr. Seuss was definitely onto something when he wrote *Green Eggs and Ham*, which became a revered childhood classic. This recipe is both tasty and healthy and will be loved by all ages. You can make it different every time by changing up your choice of green veggies and herbs. If you use pastry shells, it's ideal for a light lunch; pastry cups are perfect for serving to a crowd.

Preheat the oven to 400°F. Line a large rimmed baking sheet with parchment paper or lightly greased aluminum foil.

Separate the puff pastry shells or cups and transfer them to the prepared baking sheet. Bake for 18 to 20 minutes, until the shells are golden but slightly underdone. Remove from the oven and let cool, but keep the oven on.

Lightly whisk the eggs in a mixing bowl. Add the crème fraîche, mixed greens, and pesto. Pour the mixture into a food processor and pulse until a smooth custard forms. Return to the mixing bowl and add the chopped bacon and cheese. Season with salt and pepper.

Fill the puff pastry shells three-quarters full with the custard (about 2 tablespoons, or 1 tablespoon if using puff pastry cups), and place the shell tops alongside on the baking sheet. Bake for 20 minutes, until the shells are puffed and golden. (If you're using cups, reduce the baking time to about 10 minutes.)

Remove from the oven and let cool for a few minutes. Serve with the shell tops.

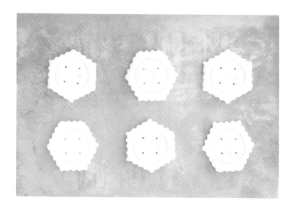

Crowd-Pleasing Mini Quiches

MAKES 12 MINI QUICHES

⏱ READY IN 45 MINUTES

1 (15-ounce) package pie crust

1 tablespoon olive oil

1 small onion, finely chopped

½ cup finely chopped multicolored
   bell pepper

Salt and pepper, to taste

4 eggs

1 cup milk

¼ cup pesto

¼ cup finely chopped parsley

2 scallions, thinly sliced

½ cup finely chopped tomato

½ cup shredded Swiss or Gruyère

NOTE: To make this even easier, you can use premade mini pie crusts from your grocery store. You can also make a crustless version of these quiches: Simply skip the directions related to the pie dough.

These mini quiches are easy to make and even easier to eat. The beauty of this dish is you can use whatever you have in your refrigerator. There is no wrong way to go! For this recipe, you will need a 3-inch round cookie cutter and two 6-cup standard muffin tins (or, if you want them super mini, a 2-inch round cookie cutter and two 12-cup mini muffin tins). If you don't have muffin tins, feel free to make this in a pie plate and serve up delicious slices to your guests. You may have to increase the cooking time.

Preheat the oven to 375°F. Spray two 6-cup muffin tins with cooking spray and set them aside.

Roll out the pie dough to approximately a 1/8-inch thickness. Using a 3-inch round cookie cutter, cut out 12 circles of pie dough. Press one dough round into each cup of the prepared muffin tins. Prick the dough several times with a fork to prevent blistering and rising. Transfer the muffin tins to the oven and parbake the dough for 3 minutes. Remove the tins from the oven and set them aside to let the dough cool slightly.

Heat the olive oil in a large nonstick skillet over medium-high heat. Add the onion, bell pepper, and a pinch each of salt and pepper. Cook the vegetables until they soften, 3 to 5 minutes. Set aside.

Whisk together the eggs, milk, pesto, parsley, scallions, and tomatoes in a bowl. Add the cooked onion and bell pepper to the mixture; season with salt and pepper.

To assemble the quiches, scatter the shredded cheese on the parbaked dough rounds. Pour the egg mixture over the cheese and fill three-quarters full. Set the muffin tins on a rimmed baking sheet and bake for 18 minutes, or until the eggs are set. Remove from the oven, and let sit for 10 minutes before serving.

Pesto Omelette Your Way

MAKES 1 SERVING

⊙ READY IN 20 MINUTES

2 eggs

1 tablespoon water

Salt and pepper, to taste

¼ cup pesto

2 scallions, thinly sliced

¼ cup shredded cheese, such as
Swiss, Emmentaler, or Gruyère

2 slices bacon, cooked (see
method on page 8) and cut into
small dice

2 tablespoons diced red bell
pepper

2 tablespoons mixed fresh herbs,
such as dill, parsley, and/or
thyme, 1 teaspoon reserved for
garnish

I was lucky enough to have Nana Dale, my mother-in-law, gift me with her vintage hinged omelette pan. This has been my way to continue the Lennox omelette tradition. If you are fortunate enough to have one of these pans in your pantry, you can use the hinged omelette pan method. If you don't, use the classic skillet recipe. Once you master the art of omelette making, the sky is the limit for pesto and filling combinations–"your way" can be different every time.

Classic Skillet Method: Crack the eggs into a large bowl. Add the water (this makes for fluffier eggs) and a pinch each of salt and pepper. Beat the eggs until well blended. Spray a nonstick skillet with cooking spray and place it over medium heat. Pour in the egg mixture and cook for a minute or two. Spread the pesto on one half of the omelette. Sprinkle the scallions, cheese, bacon, red bell pepper, and herbs on top of the pesto. Let it cook, undisturbed, for another 1 to 2 minutes. Slide a rubber spatula under the side with no ingredients and flip it onto the pesto side. Gently loosen the omelette and slide it onto your serving plate. Garnish with the reserved herbs. Serve immediately.

Hinged Omelette Pan Method: Crack the eggs into a large bowl. Add the water (this makes for fluffier eggs) and a pinch each of salt and pepper. Beat the eggs until well blended. Spray both sides of an omelette pan with cooking spray. Place it over medium heat. Pour half of the egg mixture into each side of the pan. Let it cook for a minute or two. Spread a layer of pesto on one side of the omelette, then top the pesto with the scallions, cheese, bacon, red bell pepper, and herbs. Let it cook for another 1 to 2 minutes. Fold the side with no ingredients onto the pesto mixture to close and cook for another minute. Flip it onto a plate and garnish with the reserved herbs. Serve immediately.

Avocado Pesto Toast

MAKES 4 SERVINGS

🕐 READY IN 20 MINUTES

Avocado Hummus Pesto
½ ripe avocado
¼ cup pesto
¼ cup hummus
Juice of ½ lemon
Salt and pepper, to taste

Avocado Ricotta Pesto
½ ripe avocado
¼ cup pesto
¼ cup ricotta
1 garlic clove, finely minced
Juice of ½ lime
Salt and pepper, to taste

Assembly
2 eggs
4 thick slices rustic-style bread,
   toasted
Salt, to taste
2 slices smoked salmon
Lemon wedge, for garnish
Dill sprigs, for garnish
Capers, for garnish

I create a new version of avocado toast on a weekly basis. This recipe offers two versions of avocado pesto, both of which pair nicely with smoked salmon and eggs. If you have leftovers, they make wonderful dips. Remember to purchase your avocados a few days in advance, as they need time to ripen. Feel free to change up your garnishes and go for colorful varieties, such as thinly sliced watermelon radishes, sliced scallions, or diced red onions. Our Creamy Pesto Hummus (see page 106) could easily be used in this recipe as well.

To prepare the avocado hummus pesto, combine all the ingredients in a bowl and mash together.

To prepare the avocado ricotta pesto, combine all the ingredients in a bowl and mash together.

Heat a lightly greased nonstick skillet over medium-high heat. One at a time, break the eggs and carefully slip them into the skillet. Lower the heat to low and cook the eggs slowly, until the whites have set and the yolks have started to harden. Carefully flip the eggs in the pan and cook the opposite side for 30 to 60 seconds.

To assemble, spread the avocado hummus pesto on two of the toast slices. Top each with a fried egg and sprinkle with salt. Spread the avocado ricotta pesto on the remaining two toast slices. Top each with a slice of smoked salmon and finish with a squeeze of lemon, a sprig of dill, and a few capers. Serve immediately.

Red Shakshuka

Green
Shakshuka

**PESTO
SHAKSHUKA**
page 48

Pesto Shakshuka

MAKES 4 SERVINGS
⏱ READY IN 60 MINUTES
Pictured on previous page

Shakshuka is a stewed egg dish that originated in Tunisia and has been popularized in Israeli cuisine. I became interested in creating a pesto-centric version after discovering the charming restaurant Jack's Wife Freda in Soho, New York. Its version of this Mediterranean-inspired dish was beautifully captured on Instagram feeds and even better when served in the restaurant. I am sharing two versions—a spicier green shakshuka and a slightly sweet red one. This is one of those egg dishes that works morning, noon, or night. The vibrant flavors of shakshuka are wonderful served over rice, polenta, or even a nice thick piece of crusty bread.

Green Shakshuka

1 tablespoon oil
1 medium white onion, chopped
2 garlic cloves, minced
2 cups chopped spinach
1 cup mixed herbs, such as chives, cilantro,
   and/or dill
1½ cups chopped green tomatoes or
   tomatillos
1 cup chopped mushrooms (any variety)
¼ teaspoon finely minced jalapeño
¼ cup pesto, such as spinach pesto
½ teaspoon ground turmeric
½ teaspoon ground cumin
Salt and pepper, to taste
¼ cup water
1 teaspoon lime juice
2 eggs
2 tablespoons crumbled feta, for garnish

Heat the oil in a medium nonstick skillet
over medium-high heat. Add the onion and
cook until translucent, about 5 minutes.
Add the garlic and cook, stirring, for 30
seconds. Be careful not to let it burn. Lower
the heat to medium-low. Add the spinach,
herbs, tomatoes, mushrooms, jalapeño, and
pesto, stirring to combine. Add the turmeric,
cumin, salt, pepper, water, and lime juice.
Cover the skillet and simmer for 5 minutes.

Crack the eggs into individual ramekins.
With the back of a wooden spoon, create two
shallow wells in the stew and gently slide
one egg into each well. Cover the skillet and
cook for another 8 to 10 minutes, until the
egg white is no longer runny and appears
opaque and the yolk is softly set.

To serve, carefully ladle the shakshuka into
two bowls. Garnish each evenly with the feta.

Red Shakshuka

1 tablespoon oil
1 small red onion, chopped
2 garlic cloves, minced
1 (28-ounce) can chopped tomatoes
1 cup diced red bell pepper
1 cup mixed herbs, such as basil, parsley,
   and/or chives
¼ cup pesto, such as Sun-Dried Tomato
   Pesto (page 30)
½ teaspoon sugar
¼ teaspoon ground cayenne
¼ teaspoon paprika
¼ teaspoon red pepper flakes
¼ teaspoon ground cumin
Salt and pepper, to taste
2 eggs
2 tablespoons crumbled feta, for garnish

Heat the oil in a medium nonstick skillet over
medium-high heat. Add the onion and cook
until translucent, about 5 minutes. Add the
garlic and cook, stirring, for 30 seconds. Be
careful not to let it burn. Lower the heat to
medium-low. Add the tomatoes with their
juices, bell pepper, herbs, and pesto, stirring
to combine. Add the sugar, cayenne, paprika,
red pepper flakes, cumin, salt, and pepper.
Cover the skillet and simmer for 10 minutes.

Crack the eggs into individual ramekins.
With the back of a wooden spoon, create two
shallow wells in the stew and gently slide
one egg into each well. Cover the skillet and
cook for another 8 to 10 minutes, until the
egg white is no longer runny and appears
opaque and the yolk is softly set.

To serve, carefully ladle the shakshuka into
two bowls. Garnish each evenly with the feta.

Pesto Polenta with Poached Eggs in Pepper Rounds

MAKES 6 SERVINGS

⏱ READY IN 20 MINUTES

4 cups vegetable broth
(see method on page 8),
chicken broth, or water

1 cup instant polenta

¼ cup pesto

2 tablespoons butter

1 cup grated parmesan

Salt and pepper, to taste

6 eggs

2 bell peppers (any color)

1 tablespoon olive oil

1 tablespoon water

NOTE: This dish can easily be made with creamy grits or fluffy quinoa in place of the polenta. Vary your eggs as well–fried one day, baked the next, and poached on the weekend.

If you are looking for a healthy twist and a fun way to present your poached eggs, try this velvety, rich, cheese-spiked creamy polenta recipe and feel like you are indulging without any of the guilt.

In a large saucepan, bring the broth to a boil over medium-high heat. Pour in the polenta and, whisking continuously, cook until it boils and begins to thicken. Cover, lower the heat to medium-low, and simmer, whisking periodically, for about 5 minutes, until the polenta is smooth and all the liquid has been absorbed. Polenta cooking times may vary, so follow the package instructions. Add the pesto, butter, and cheese and stir until the mixture is creamy. Taste and season with salt and pepper. Set aside.

Crack the eggs into individual ramekins and set aside.

Slice each pepper crosswise through its widest section into three ½-inch-thick rounds; remove the ribs and seeds. (Reserve the remainder of each pepper for another use.)

Heat the oil in a large nonstick skillet over medium-high heat. Place the pepper rounds evenly spaced in the skillet and cook for 2 minutes on one side. Flip the pepper rounds, then slide an egg into each pepper round. Don't worry if the egg spills over the sides of the pepper; it will still be delicious! Season with salt and pepper. Let the eggs cook for 1 minute, add the water to the pan, cover, and cook for another 3 to 4 minutes for a softer egg. Add an additional 2 minutes for a well-done egg.

To serve, divide the pesto polenta evenly among six bowls and top each with a pepper-poached egg.

Pastas and Pizzas

There's no substitute for a hot, crispy pizza fresh out of a wood-burning oven or a hearty, steaming bowl of pasta at your favorite trattoria. If your schedule does not allow a trip out, get the same enjoyment at home in one hour or less. Learn how to combine pesto and other ingredients to prepare pastas and pizzas that are classic with a modern spin. Try vegetable-based crusts for your pizza, or make a personal pizza using naan for an international spin. All while garnering rave reviews!

Spicy Thai-Inspired Noodles

MAKES 4 SERVINGS
⊙ READY IN 45 MINUTES

4 ounces long, thin pasta, such as
  capellini
1 cup shredded or spiralized carrot
  noodles (see method on page 9)
1 cup shredded or spiralized daikon
  radish noodles (see method no
  page 9; optional)
1 teaspoon peanut oil
1 cup ½-inch tofu cubes
2 garlic cloves, minced
1 teaspoon minced fresh ginger
¼ cup thinly sliced red onion
⅔ cup sugar snap peas, blanched
½ small jalapeño, diced
½ cup chopped cilantro leaves
1 cup Thai-Inspired Pesto
  Vinaigrette (page 26)
2 scallions, white parts only, thinly
  sliced, for garnish
¼ cup whole or crushed peanuts,
  for garnish

In this recipe, East meets West. Instead of using traditional rice noodles (which of course you can), I substituted Italian pasta and the results were excellent. For this dish, I encourage you to be creative and use a Thai-inspired pesto for a colorful and light yet satisfying meal.

Bring a large pot of salted water to a boil. Add the pasta and cook according to package instructions. Drain the pasta, transfer it to a large bowl, and add the carrot noodles and daikon radish noodles (if using).

Warm the oil in a wok or nonstick skillet over high heat, swirling the oil so that it coats the wok. You will know the wok is ready when you flick a drop of water into the oil and it sizzles. Add the tofu and stir-fry until it is golden in spots, 7 to 10 minutes. Add the garlic and ginger and stir-fry for 30 seconds. Be careful not to let it burn.

Transfer the tofu mixture to the pasta bowl. Add the red onion, sugar snap peas, jalapeño, and cilantro. Pour in the vinaigrette a little at a time to find the perfect balance, tossing to combine. Garnish with the scallions and peanuts and serve right away, or let rest in the bowl at room temperature for about 30 minutes to let the flavors develop and deepen.

Pesto Lasagna

MAKES 6 SERVINGS

⏱ READY IN 90 MINUTES

1 (15-ounce) container ricotta
cheese

1 egg

2½ cups shredded mozzarella,
divided

½ cup pesto, divided

¼ teaspoon dried oregano

Salt and pepper, to taste

1 tablespoon olive oil

½ cup chopped onion

1 garlic clove, minced

1 (28-ounce) jar tomato sauce

12 no-boil lasagna noodles

1¼ cups sliced or torn mozzarella

NOTE: For a riff on a classic
lasagna, use soaked and
softened ruffle-edged dried
lasagna noodles, and roll
up all the ingredients into
individual lasagna rolls.

I love making lasagna, especially when it can be made so easily using no-boil noodles. Pesto is my secret ingredient to enhance the flavor of the creamy ricotta cheese, and the two types of mozzarella contribute different textures. I have made this lasagna in many different iterations: meat, sausage or completely vegetarian. It never fails! You can prepare your lasagna in advance and refrigerate it for up to 2 days; just bring it to room temperature before putting it in the oven. For a fun, healthier spin on lasagna, try substituting eggplant or zucchini slices for the oven-ready noodles.

Preheat the oven to 375°F. Move the oven rack to the middle position. Lightly grease a 9 × 13-inch baking dish and set it aside.

Mix together the ricotta, egg, 1 cup of the shredded mozzarella, ¼ cup of the pesto, the oregano, and salt and pepper in a large bowl. Set aside.

Heat the olive oil in a large saucepan over medium-high heat. Add the onion and cook, stirring occasionally, until translucent, about 5 minutes. Add the garlic and cook, stirring, for 30 seconds. Be careful not to let it burn. Stir in the tomato sauce, lower the heat to low, and simmer for about 5 minutes. Set the tomato mixture aside to cool for 5 minutes.

Spread ½ cup of the tomato sauce in the bottom of the prepared baking dish and top with 3 lasagna sheets. Spread one-third of the ricotta-pesto mixture on top, then add ½ cup of the tomato sauce, ½ cup of the shredded mozzarella, and 1/3 cup of the torn mozzarella. Repeat this process to make three more layers, starting with the lasagna sheets and ending with the remaining sauce and shredded and torn mozzarella. Dot the remaining ¼ cup pesto over the top.

Cover the dish with aluminum foil and transfer it to the oven. Bake for 50 minutes. Remove the foil and bake for another 5 minutes. Let the lasagna cool for 10 minutes before serving.

Baked Pesto Risotto

MAKES 4 SERVINGS
⏱ READY IN 60 MINUTES

1 tablespoon olive oil
1 cup chopped white onion
2 garlic cloves, minced
1 cup Arborio rice
½ cup dry white wine
2 cups vegetable broth (see method on page 8), chicken broth, or water
¼ cup pesto, plus 2 tablespoons for garnish
2 tablespoons chopped herbs, such as thyme, oregano, and/or parsley
¼ cup grated parmesan, plus 2 tablespoons for garnish
½ teaspoon grated lemon zest
Salt and pepper, to taste

NOTE: Experiment with different broths (vegetable, chicken, turkey, or fish) and different wine profiles to make the risotto unique each time. Of course, the same goes with the flavor of pesto you select!

I made risotto often when Dave and I were first married. I would stand over the stovetop for over an hour, stirring the broth into the rice. Today, with a few simple ingredients, one Dutch oven, and one-quarter the time at the stove, you can make your creamy risotto in the oven while you relax with your guests. This risotto is wonderful on its own. For a heartier dish, try adding some cooked meat or roasted vegetables.

Preheat the oven to 375°F.

Warm the olive oil in a Dutch oven over medium heat. Add the onion and cook, stirring occasionally, until translucent, about 5 minutes. Add the garlic and cook, stirring, for 30 seconds. Be careful not to let it burn. Add the rice and cook, stirring, until it turns from opaque white to slightly translucent, about 3 minutes. Add the wine and let it evaporate slightly and absorb into the rice, about 5 minutes. Add the broth and simmer for 5 minutes. Cover the Dutch oven and transfer to the oven. Bake for 30 minutes, or until the rice is tender.

Stir in the pesto, herbs, cheese, and lemon zest. Season with salt and pepper. Garnish with the additional parmesan and pesto before serving.

Butternut Squash Ravioli with Pesto Sauce

MAKES 4 SERVINGS
⏱ READY IN 45 MINUTES

1 small butternut squash, peeled, seeded, and cut into ½-inch cubes (about 1 cup)
2 tablespoons olive oil, divided
Salt and pepper, to taste
¼ cup mascarpone or sour cream
1 teaspoon lemon juice
1 tablespoon thinly sliced scallions, white parts only
20 square wonton wrappers
Parmesan cheese, for garnish

Pesto Sauce
2 tablespoons olive oil
½ cup pesto
Juice of 1 lemon

NOTE: You can prepare the ravioli in advance. Simply place the baking sheet with the uncooked ravioli in the freezer for about 2 hours. Transfer them to a zip-top freezer bag, and store in the freezer for up to 2 weeks. Pull out these frozen delights whenever you like, and cook for 3 to 5 minutes in boiling water.

Not everyone has the time and patience to make pasta dough from scratch for delicious homemade ravioli. That is why I recommend the next best thing: wonton wrappers. Their size makes a perfect substitute; add a delicious filling, and these little raviolis become works of art. Each bite is filled with a lush, creamy jolt of flavor.

Preheat the oven to 375°F. Line two large rimmed baking sheets with parchment paper.

Toss the squash with 1 tablespoon of the olive oil on one of the prepared baking sheets. Season with salt and pepper. Spread out into a single layer and roast for 25 minutes, or until the squash is golden and soft. Remove the baking sheet from the oven and let the squash cool slightly.

Transfer the roasted squash to a food processor. Add the mascarpone, lemon juice, scallions, and remaining 1 tablespoon olive oil, as well as more salt and pepper as needed. Pulse until smooth; set aside.

Fill a small bowl with water. Place one wonton wrapper on a clean, dry work surface. Dip your finger in the water and gently dampen the outer edge of the wrapper. Be careful not to use too much water, as your wrappers will become soggy quickly. Place 1½ teaspoons of the squash filling in the center of the wrapper and fold it over diagonally into a triangle, pressing on the edges to create a seal. Then, fold the two outer corners into the center so that they overlap, and press together. Transfer the ravioli to the second prepared baking pan and cover it with a damp towel so the ravioli do not dry out. Repeat this process with the remaining wrappers and filling.

To make the pesto sauce, heat the oil in a medium saucepan over medium-low heat. Add the pesto and lemon juice, stirring to combine. Let the sauce simmer as you cook the ravioli.

Bring a large pot of salted water to a boil. Working in batches, gently slide the ravioli into the boiling water, making sure not to crowd the pot, and cook for about 3 minutes, until the ravioli float to the surface and look translucent. Transfer them to a plate lined with paper towels while you wait for the rest to cook.

To serve, place five ravioli on each plate and drizzle the pesto sauce on top. Garnish with parmesan.

**PESTO PASTA
TRILOGY** *page 62*

Roasted Broccoli
Orecchiette

Fennel
Capellini

Roasted Beet and
Blood Orange
Pappardelle

Pesto Pasta Trilogy

MAKES 12 SERVINGS

⏲ READY IN 60 TO 90 MINUTES

Pictured on previous page

Offering pastas of various colors, widths, and shapes makes for a beautiful party presentation. In the following recipes, I suggest orecchiette, pappardelle, and capellini, but feel free to use whatever pasta shapes you enjoy and have on hand. It pays to be organized when preparing all three at one time. After you have finished roasting your vegetables, make sure to turn the oven to a low setting (around 200°F) and place your prepared pasta in the oven while you are completing them one by one. Or, if you have warming trays or chafing dishes, place the prepared pasta (covered with aluminum foil) on top so that the temperature will be maintained. Lastly, you can always pop the pasta into the microwave on a low setting. Just make sure you are using a microwave-safe dish. When it is time for your guests to arrive, all three dishes will be warm and ready to enjoy.

Roasted Broccoli Orecchiette

1 large head broccoli, cut into florets (about 3 cups)
2 tablespoons olive oil, divided
Salt and pepper, to taste
8 ounces orecchiette
¼ cup pesto, such as broccoli stem pesto
Red pepper flakes, for garnish

Preheat the oven to 400°F. Line a large rimmed baking sheet with parchment paper or lightly greased aluminum foil.

Toss the broccoli florets with 1 tablespoon of the olive oil on the prepared baking sheet. Season with salt and pepper. Spread out into a single layer and roast for 20 minutes.

Meanwhile, bring a large pot of salted water to a boil. Add the orecchiette and cook according to package instructions. Reserve 1 cup of the pasta water, then drain the pasta and set aside.

Warm the remaining 1 tablespoon olive oil in a nonstick skillet over medium-low heat. Add the pasta, roasted broccoli, and pesto, tossing together until everything is heated through and the flavors are blended. If the pasta seems dry, add some of the reserved pasta water.

Season with salt and pepper. Transfer the pasta to a warm serving dish and garnish with red pepper flakes.

Roasted Beet and Blood Orange Pappardelle

2 small beets
1 tablespoon water
8 ounces pappardelle
1 tablespoon olive oil
1 blood orange, cut into segments
¼ cup pesto, such as beet greens pesto
Salt and pepper, to taste
1 tablespoon crumbled goat cheese, for garnish
Crushed sweet and spicy pecans, for garnish

Preheat the oven to 400°F.

Place the beets on a sheet of aluminum foil and add the water. Fold up the foil to enclose the beets in a tight packet. Place the packet on a small rimmed baking sheet and roast for 30 to 45 minutes, or until a knife easily pierces the beets. Set the wrapped beets aside until they are cool enough to handle. Wearing rubber gloves to avoid staining your hands, remove and discard the skin from the beets, which should easily peel off. Cut the beets into ¼-inch cubes.

Meanwhile, bring a large pot of salted water to a boil. Add the pappardelle and cook according to package instructions. Reserve 1 cup of the pasta water, then drain the pasta and set aside.

Warm the oil in a nonstick skillet over medium-low heat. Add the pasta, roasted beets, orange segments, and pesto, tossing together until everything is heated through and the flavors are blended. If the pasta seems dry, add some of the reserved pasta water.

Season with salt and pepper. Transfer the pasta to a warm serving dish and garnish with the goat cheese and pecans.

Fennel Capellini

8 ounces capellini
1 tablespoon olive oil
1 fennel bulb, thinly sliced (about 2 cups), plus its fronds
¼ cup pesto, such as lemon pesto
Salt and pepper, to taste
Grated lemon zest, for garnish

Bring a large pot of salted water to a boil. Add the capellini and cook according to package instructions. Reserve 1 cup of the pasta water, then drain the pasta and set aside.

Warm the oil in a nonstick skillet over medium heat. Add the fennel and fronds and cook, stirring occasionally, until slightly wilted and browned in spots, 7 to 10 minutes. Add the pasta and pesto, tossing together until everything is heated through and the flavors are blended. If the pasta seems dry, add some of the reserved pasta water.

Season with salt and pepper. Transfer the pasta to a warm serving dish and garnish with the lemon zest.

Ode to ABC Pizza

MAKES 6 SERVINGS

⏱ READY IN 30 MINUTES

1 (1-pound) pizza dough, at room
    temperature

Olive oil, for drizzling

1 pound brussels sprouts

1 teaspoon grated lemon zest, plus
    more to taste

Salt and pepper, to taste

Pinch red pepper flakes

½ cup ricotta cheese

¼ cup Kale Pesto (page 31)

¼ cup pancetta cubes

⅓ cup sliced and torn mozzarella
    (about 3 ounces)

2 teaspoons grated Parmigiano
    Reggiano

I have my daughter, Hope, to thank for this recipe. One of her favorite spots in New York is ABC Carpet & Home in the Flatiron District. This design emporium showcases two fabulous restaurants owned by French-American chef Jean-Georges Vongerichten, ABC Kitchen and abcV. On our first visit, Hope selected their brussels sprouts pizza with a ricotta and lemon zest base. It is amazing! Every time we go back and it is on the menu, you can bet that one of us will order it. Since it is not always available, I decided to create my own version at home. For those of you who aren't brussels sprouts fans, make sure you give this recipe a try. When these baby cabbages are cooked quickly at high heat, they turn crunchy and sweet. This pizza never disappoints!

Place a pizza stone in the upper third of a cold oven and preheat to 450°F. If you do not have a pizza stone, preheat the oven to 450°F and lightly grease a large rimmed baking sheet.

Turn out the dough onto a floured surface. Use your fingers to stretch the dough or use a rolling pin to form it into a thin 12-inch circle (or any shape you like). Transfer the dough to the pizza stone in the oven or the prepared baking sheet. Bake for 5 minutes, or until the crust is beginning to turn light golden brown. If you are using a pizza stone, carefully remove the parcooked crust from the oven and flip it over onto a clean, flat surface. If you are using a baking sheet, flip the crust back onto the baking sheet. Drizzle the crust with olive oil and set it aside while you prepare the toppings.

Using a mandoline or a very sharp knife, thinly slice the brussels sprouts. You should end up with about 2 cups. Toss the brussels sprouts in a large bowl with the lemon zest, salt, pepper, and red pepper flakes. Set aside.

In a small bowl, mix the ricotta cheese and pesto. Spread the pesto ricotta on the pizza crust, leaving a ¼-inch edge all the way around. Scatter the seasoned brussels sprouts on top, then top with the pancetta cubes and mozzarella. Sprinkle the Parmigiano Reggiano over all. Add a little more lemon zest, if desired, and season with salt and pepper.

Carefully return the prepared pizza to the pizza stone in the oven, or return the baking sheet to the oven. Bake the pizza for 8 to 10 minutes, until the top is crispy. Remove the pizza from the oven and let it rest for a few minutes, then slice and serve.

Naan Pizza with Fig and Jalapeño Pesto

MAKES 4 SERVINGS
⊙ READY IN 20 MINUTES

4 (8 × 4-inch) pieces naan bread

¼ teaspoon dried cilantro

⅛ teaspoon ground cumin

¼ teaspoon salt

¼ teaspoon pepper

4 tablespoons pesto

4 tablespoons feta

2 jalapeños, roasted (see method on page 6) and cut into small chunks

4 tablespoons cilantro or parsley, divided

1 cup fresh figs, sliced, quartered, or halved

Fresh diced raw jalapeño, to garnish

Naan is a traditional Indian flatbread. Today, it is easy to find at your local supermarket in many different flavors. Choose your favorite—all will work perfectly for this recipe. I discovered figs were the perfect partner to pesto when we lived in Atlanta. We had a stand of fig trees in our backyard and had to find ways to eat them before the birds did! If you are unable to find fresh figs, use dried figs. You may want to soak them for a few minutes in warm water to hydrate them.

Preheat the oven to 400°F. Line a large rimmed baking sheet with parchment paper.

Place the naan on the prepared baking sheet.

Combine the dried cilantro, cumin, salt, and pepper. Spread 1 tablespoon of the pesto over each piece of naan. Evenly distribute the feta, roasted jalapeños, cilantro, figs, and spice mixture over the pesto.

Bake the pizza for 12 minutes, until the naan is golden brown. Garnish with raw jalapeño and serve.

Sweet Roasted Date Flatbread

MAKES 4 SERVINGS

⊙ READY IN 20 MINUTES

4 (6-inch) round flatbreads

4 tablespoons pesto

1½ cups arugula

2 slices prosciutto, torn into small pieces

4 tablespoons crumbled goat cheese

10 to 12 dates, thinly sliced (about ½ cup)

⅓ cup chopped pitted Kalamata olives

Salt and pepper, to taste

You will no longer need to run to your artisan pizza shop when you are in the mood for something different. The salty-sweet flavors of this flatbread will save you time and money. Get out of your dinner rut with a reinvented way to serve pizza.

Preheat the oven to 400°F. Line a large rimmed baking sheet with parchment paper.

Place the flatbreads on the prepared baking sheet. On each flatbread, spread 1 tablespoon of the pesto. Evenly divide the arugula, prosciutto, goat cheese, dates, and olives on top of the pesto. Season with salt and pepper.

Bake the flatbreads for 8 to 10 minutes, until the prosciutto is crispy and the arugula has wilted slightly. Serve.

BOUNTIFUL CAULIFLOWER CRUST PIZZA
page 73

Bountiful Cauliflower Crust Pizza

MAKES 4 SERVINGS

⏱ READY IN 30 MINUTES

Pictured on previous page

1 (10-ounce) cauliflower crust
2 tablespoons pancetta cubes
½ red bell pepper, thinly sliced
½ small onion, thinly sliced
6-8 mushrooms (any variety),
    thinly sliced (about 1 cup)
½ teaspoon dried oregano
Salt and pepper, to taste
2 tablespoons pesto
2 tablespoons ricotta cheese
½ cup shredded mozzarella
½ cup grated parmesan

NOTE: This vegetable crust pizza pairs beautifully with a thinly sliced fennel salad with mandarin orange segments, as pictured here.

Gone are the days when you are limited to a dough-based pizza. Today, pizza crusts are made with just about anything you can think of. My favorite is a cauliflower crust pizza piled high with toppings. If you think you don't like cauliflower, I urge you to give this a try. You will be a convert in no time! I now buy cauliflower pizza crust in quantity, and I'm always only 30 minutes away from making a healthy meal for my family. You can find them in the freezer section of most grocery stores.

Preheat the oven to 450°F. Line a large rimmed baking sheet with parchment paper.

Place the cauliflower crust on the prepared baking sheet. Bake for 12 minutes. Remove the baking sheet from the oven, carefully flip over the crust, and set aside.

While the pizza crust is baking, warm a nonstick skillet over medium-high heat. Add the pancetta, bell pepper, onion, mushrooms, oregano, salt, and pepper and cook, stirring occasionally, for about 5 minutes, until all the vegetables have softened. Set the vegetable mixture aside.

Combine the pesto and ricotta. Spread the pesto mixture on the cauliflower crust. Add the sautéed vegetable mixture. Top with the mozzarella and parmesan.

Bake the pizza for about 12 minutes, until the cheese is melted and bubbly. Let the pizza rest for a few minutes before cutting it into slices and serving.

Caprese Calzone

MAKES 4 SERVINGS

⏱ READY IN 30 MINUTES

1 (1-pound) pizza dough, at room
   temperature
1 cup tomato sauce
4 tablespoons pesto
1 cup shredded mozzarella
Salt and pepper, to taste
1 tablespoon olive oil
Grated parmesan, for garnish

A calzone is simply a folded pizza. The advantage of a calzone is that the ingredients are held together in a neat little package. Once you try this recipe, you will be making calzones time and time again. The hardest part may be trying to decide what combination of flavors you will try next! I suggest serving these calzones with a side salad of arugula and grape tomatoes.

Place a pizza stone in the upper third of a cold oven and preheat to 450°F. If you do not have a pizza stone, preheat the oven to 450°F and lightly grease a large rimmed baking sheet.

Divide the pizza dough into four equal pieces. On a lightly floured surface, roll each piece of dough into a 6-inch circle using a rolling pin. If your dough offers resistance, let it rest for a few minutes and try rolling again.

To assemble, moisten the outer edge of one dough round with water. Spread ¼ cup of the tomato sauce across half of each round, leaving a ¼-inch edge all the way around. Add 1 tablespoon of the pesto and ¼ cup of the mozzarella to the sauced side. Season with salt and pepper. Fold the dough over into a half-moon shape and, using the tines of a fork, press the edges to create a seal. Repeat this process with the remaining dough rounds and filling.

Brush the olive oil over the top of each calzone. With a sharp knife, make two or three slits on the top of each calzone to allow steam to escape. Dust them with parmesan and transfer them to the pizza stone or the prepared baking sheet. Bake the calzones for 18 minutes, or until they are golden and crispy. Transfer them to a cooling rack and let cool for a few minutes before serving. Don't worry if some of the filling has spilled out. Embrace the imperfections!

Sandwiches, Paninis, Bruschetta, and Crostini

Sandwiches have always been a staple of the Hope's Gardens kitchen. Whether enjoyed poolside or over a farmer's table with friends, they offer a straightforward means of combining delicious and diverse odds and ends with little fuss. This chapter celebrates the elegant simplicity of sandwiches, paninis, bruschetta, and crostini for one or a crowd.

Rainbow
Pesto Tea
Sandwiches

Open-Faced
Cucumber Pesto
Sandwiches

Open-Faced Red
Radish and Pesto
Sandwiches

Pesto Tea Sandwiches

MAKES 6 TO 8 SERVINGS
⏱ READY IN 60 MINUTES

Wondering what to serve at your next book club gathering or Mother's Day brunch? Look no further than these charming pesto tea sandwiches. They come together with minimal effort, and your guests will think you spent all day in the kitchen. I have offered a few suggestions, but don't be limited by these recommendations. Feel free to use your imagination to create your own versions of these tea sandwiches. The possibilities are endless. For a beautiful presentation, try laying out all your sandwiches on a cake platter or a wooden cutting board. Remember that the secret to a great gathering is not only great food but great presentation as well!

Egg Salad and Pesto Tea Sandwiches

Open-Faced Smoked Salmon Pesto Sandwiches

Rainbow Pesto Tea Sandwiches

16 slices very thin white bread, crusts removed

4 teaspoons pesto, such as Classic Basil Pesto (page 23)

4 teaspoons pesto, such as Sun-Dried Tomato Pesto (page 30)

4 teaspoons pesto, such as Roasted Jalapeño–Cilantro Pesto (page 30)

8 olives, pitted

8 cherry or grape tomatoes

Lay out four slices of bread. On one slice, spread 1 teaspoon of the first pesto, and top it with the second slice of bread. Spread 1 teaspoon of the second flavor of pesto on that slice of bread, and top it with the third slice of bread. Spread on 1 teaspoon of the third flavor of pesto, and top with the remaining slice of bread. Cut the sandwich on the diagonal and insert a toothpick threaded with one olive and one tomato to decorate each half. Repeat this process with the remaining bread, pesto, olives, and tomatoes.

Keep your sandwiches simple. No fancy ingredients needed! Ideally, each guest will sample four to six sandwiches. Lastly, don't overfill them.

Egg Salad and Pesto Tea Sandwiches

8 slices very thin white bread, crusts removed
4 tablespoons pesto, such as parsley pesto
4 tablespoons egg salad
Celery leaves, for garnish

Lay out four slices of bread. Spread 1 table-spoon pesto on each slice. Top with 1 table-spoon egg salad and finish with the remaining slices of bread. Cut the sandwiches on the diagonal and garnish each with a celery leaf.

Open-Faced Cucumber Pesto Sandwiches

4 tablespoons pesto, such as dill pesto
4 tablespoons crumbled goat cheese
4 slices pumpernickel cocktail bread
½ cucumber, thinly sliced
Chopped dill, for garnish
Salt, to taste

Mix the pesto and goat cheese together. Spread 1 tablespoon of the pesto mixture on each bread slice (you may not need it all). Top with overlapping cucumber slices and finish with dill and salt. Cut in half lengthwise.

Open-Faced Red Radish and Pesto Sandwiches

4 tablespoons pesto, such as radish greens pesto
4 tablespoons cream cheese
4 slices very thin white bread, crusts removed
2 red radishes, thinly sliced
Finely minced red onion, for garnish

Mix the pesto and cream cheese together. Spread 1 tablespoon of the pesto cream on each bread slice (you may not need it all). Top with overlapping radish slices and garnish with red onion. Cut in half lengthwise.

Open-Faced Smoked Salmon Pesto Sandwiches

8 teaspoons pesto, such as chive pesto
8 slices pumpernickel cocktail bread
2 slices smoked salmon, each cut into 4 pieces
Minced chives, to garnish
Squeeze of lemon, to garnish

Spread 1 teaspoon pesto on each slice of bread, then top with a slice of smoked salmon. Garnish with chives and a squeeze of lemon juice. Cut in half diagonally.

The Gouda Goodness BLAT

MAKES 4 SERVINGS
⏱ READY IN 10 MINUTES

1 ripe avocado, peeled and pitted
¼ cup pesto
8 (½-inch-thick) slices bread
8 slices Gouda
8 slices bacon, cooked
    (see method on page 8)
    and halved crosswise
1 cup shredded lettuce
8 slices tomato

NOTE: If you desire extra pesto goodness, look for pesto Gouda in the specialty cheese section of your grocery store.

This sandwich combines all my favorite things: bacon, lettuce, avocado, tomatoes (BLAT), and of course, pesto and cheese. Treat yourself to this decadent sandwich that will be ready in under 10 minutes!

Heat a panini press. If you don't have a panini press, you can use a nonstick skillet on the stovetop.

Mash the avocado and pesto together in a bowl.

Spread 1 tablespoon of the avocado pesto on each slice of bread. Top each with a slice of Gouda, two half-slices of bacon, 2 tablespoons of shredded lettuce, and a tomato slice.

Press two topped bread slices together, making one extra-stuffed sandwich. Repeat with the remaining slices.

Lightly mist the outsides of each sandwich with cooking oil spray. Transfer the sandwiches, one or two at a time, to the panini press and cook for 3 minutes, or until the cheese is melted and the bread is golden. If you are using a nonstick skillet, warm it over medium-high heat, spray with cooking oil spray, and place your sandwich in the pan. Using a heavy pot, apply pressure and press your sandwich for about 3 minutes, until a nice crust forms. Flip the sandwich and cook for another 3 minutes with the pot on top.

Let the sandwiches cool for 1 minute, halve diagonally, and serve.

Mediterranean Roasted Veggie Sandwich

MAKES 4 SERVINGS

○ **READY IN 40 MINUTES**

4 cups sliced or chopped
  vegetables, such as bell
  peppers, zucchini, butternut
  squash, eggplant, and/or onion
1 tablespoon olive oil
Salt and pepper, to taste
4 tablespoons Pesto Mayo
  (page 27)
4 focaccia rolls, halved
4 tablespoons hummus
4 slices fontina

NOTE: If you have not made our
Creamy Pesto Hummus (see page
106), please try it in this recipe.

Roasted vegetables are a staple in our home because they're
so easy to prepare. In this recipe, it really doesn't matter what
vegetables you roast, as they will undoubtedly play a starring
role and be delicious. Eat this as is, or use a panini press to
heat the sandwich until the cheese is gooey and melted.

Preheat the oven to 400°F. Line two medium or large rimmed
baking sheets with parchment paper or lightly greased aluminum foil.

Put the vegetables in a large bowl. Add the olive oil, season
with salt and pepper, and mix everything with your hands until
all the vegetables are evenly coated with oil. Transfer them to
the prepared baking sheets, making sure to arrange them so
that no pieces are touching. (This helps the vegetables roast
and not steam.) Roast for about 30 minutes, checking midway
through to make sure they are not burning, until the vegetables are tender and caramelized.

To assemble the sandwiches, spread 1 tablespoon pesto mayo
on one side of each roll and 1 tablespoon hummus on the other
side. Add 1 cup of the roasted vegetables and a slice of fontina,
then close the sandwiches. If you are using a panini press, heat
and cook for about 5 minutes, until the cheese has melted and
you have beautiful grill marks on top. Serve.

Green Goddess Pesto Grilled Cheese

MAKES 4 SERVINGS

⏱ READY IN 20 MINUTES

8 tablespoons Green Goddess Pesto (page 32)

4 rustic-style rolls, halved

8 lettuce leaves

8 slices green tomato

8 slices provolone

Salt and pepper, to taste

I love the robust flavors—herbs, anchovies, and lots of garlic—of green goddess dressing, so I created the same wonderful flavors in pesto form. If you want something bold and tasty, look no further!

Heat a panini press. If you don't have a panini press, you can use a nonstick skillet on the stovetop.

Spread 1 tablespoon pesto on each side of each roll. Layer the bottom side of each with two lettuce leaves, two tomato slices, and two provolone slices. Season with salt and pepper. Close the sandwiches.

Lightly mist the outsides of each sandwich with cooking oil spray. Transfer the sandwiches, one or two at a time, to the panini press and cook for about 5 minutes, until the rolls are golden brown and the cheese has melted. If you are using a nonstick skillet, warm it over medium-high heat, spray with cooking oil spray, and place your sandwich in the pan. Using a heavy pot, apply pressure and press your sandwich for about 3 minutes, until a nice crust forms. Flip the sandwich and cook for another 3 minutes with the pot on top. Serve.

Philadelphia Cheese Steak Pesto Wraps

MAKES 4 SERVINGS
⏱ READY IN 20 MINUTES

1 (1-pound) New York strip steak

Salt and pepper, to taste

1 tablespoon olive oil

1 onion, thinly sliced

1 red bell pepper, seeded and
thinly sliced

¼ cup pesto, such as Mint Pesto
(page 31)

½ cup plain Greek yogurt

2 teaspoons thinly sliced mint
leaves

1 teaspoon lemon juice

4 pita or flatbread wraps

4 slices Havarti

I had my first cheese steak long ago, when my sister, Nancy, was a student in Philadelphia. I was in high school and would take the train from New York to spend the weekend discovering the city and learning what college was all about. My update of this classic sandwich is reinterpreted with a Greek twist. The mint and yogurt sauce lends a cool finishing touch.

Line a large rimmed baking sheet with parchment paper. Place a cast iron grill pan in a cold oven and preheat the oven to 500°F. When the oven reaches 500°F, carefully remove the grill pan and turn the oven down to 325°F.

Set the grill pan over high heat on the stovetop and spray it with cooking oil spray. Meanwhile, season both sides of the steak with salt and pepper. Grill the steak for 2 minutes, then flip and grill the other side for 2 minutes. Flip two more times (8 minutes total); an instant-read thermometer inserted into the thickest part of the steak should register 135°F for medium-rare. Transfer the steak to a cutting board, and let rest for 10 minutes before thinly slicing it.

Heat the oil in a nonstick skillet over medium-high heat. Add the onion and bell pepper. Cook, stirring frequently, until the onion has caramelized, 5 to 7 minutes. Remove the skillet from the heat.

Mix the pesto, yogurt, mint, and lemon juice together.

Lay the wraps on the prepared baking sheet. Divide the cheese, sliced steak, and sautéed onions and peppers evenly among the wraps. Drizzle each with the pesto-yogurt sauce. Bake the wraps for 5 minutes, or until the cheese is melted.

Remove the wraps from the oven, fold, and serve.

The Day after Thanksgiving Sandwich

MAKES 4 SERVINGS
◷ READY IN 20 MINUTES

½ cup Pesto Mayo (page 27)
8 slices bread
8 slices turkey breast
4 tablespoons cranberry sauce
4 slices bacon, cooked
  (see method on page 8)
  and halved crosswise
4 slices cheese (any variety)

NOTE: If you don't have any left-over cranberry sauce from your Thanksgiving dinner, here's how to make a quick version. In a small saucepan over medium heat, combine 1 (12-ounce) package fresh or frozen cranberries, the juice of 1 orange, and ¼ cup sugar. The cranberries will begin to pop after about 5 minutes. At that point, reduce the heat and let the mixture cook for several minutes. When the sauce has thickened, remove it from the heat and let it cool.

This day is special for me, as it often falls on my mother's birthday and gives us another reason to celebrate. We used to converge in Atlanta for Thanksgiving, and my parents would drive down from New York to spend the holiday with us. Dave would be in charge of roasting our turkey. He learned everything he knows about this job from our "copilot," Martha Stewart. There were always tons of leftovers; with this in mind, I created this sandwich. As we all know, a turkey dinner goes a long way!

Preheat a panini press. If you don't have a panini press, you can use a nonstick skillet on the stovetop.

Spread 1 tablespoon pesto mayo on each bread slice. Top four of the slices with two turkey slices, 1 tablespoon cranberry sauce, two half-slices of bacon, and a slice of cheese. Close the sandwiches with the remaining bread slices.

Lightly mist the outsides of each sandwich with cooking oil spray. Transfer the sandwiches, one or two at a time, to the panini press and cook until the bread is golden and the cheese is melted, 3 to 5 minutes.

Cut each sandwich on the diagonal and serve.

Roasted Lemon
and Pesto
Crostini

Spicy Pesto
Shrimp
Bruschetta

Kale Pesto
and Shiitake
Mushroom
Crostini

Roasted
Carrot
Bruschetta

Pesto Crostini and Bruschetta Party

MAKES 8 SERVINGS (5 PIECES EACH)
⏱ READY IN 90 MINUTES

The biggest difference between crostini and bruschetta is their size. Crostini tends to be smaller and thinner, and bruschetta is made from thicker, more rustic bread, which typically has a thick, heavy crust and an open texture that reminds you of a homemade loaf. These recipes are the secrets to stress-free entertaining. Set everything out ahead of time and let your guests mix and mingle, while sampling some of these delicious breads. Plan on a minimum of five hors d'oeuvres per person.

Kale Pesto and Shiitake Mushroom Crostini

16 (½-inch-thick) slices baguette
2 tablespoons olive oil
2 tablespoons butter
2 garlic cloves, finely minced
2 cups chopped shiitake mushrooms
Salt and pepper, to taste
½ cup Kale Pesto (page 31)
Grated or shaved Parmigiano Reggiano, for garnish

Preheat the oven to 325°F.

Place the baguette slices on a large rimmed baking sheet and toast for 2 minutes. Flip the slices over and toast for another 2 minutes. Remove the baking sheet from the oven and set aside.

Heat the oil and butter in a nonstick skillet over medium heat. Add the garlic and mushrooms and cook, stirring occasionally, for 5 to 7 minutes, until the mushrooms are tender and release their juices. Season with salt and pepper. Remove from the heat.

Spread 1½ teaspoons pesto on each baguette slice. Top with 1 tablespoon cooked mushrooms. Garnish the crostini with Parmigiano Reggiano.

Roasted Lemon and Pesto Crostini

16 (½-inch-thick) slices baguette
4 Meyer lemons, each cut into 4 slices (you can use regular lemons, but they will not be as sweet)
2 tablespoons olive oil
2 tablespoons sugar
½ cup pesto, such as lemon pesto
Honey, for garnish
Salt, to taste

Preheat the oven to 325°F.

Place the baguette slices on a large rimmed baking sheet and toast for 2 minutes. Flip the slices over and toast for another 2 minutes. Remove the baking sheet from the oven and set aside. Turn on the broiler.

Place the lemon slices on another large baking sheet. Brush the tops with half of the olive oil and sprinkle with half of the sugar. Broil for 3 minutes, then flip the lemon slices, brush them with the remaining oil, and sprinkle with the remaining sugar. Broil for another 3 minutes, or until the lemon slices are slightly charred and caramelized.

To assemble the crostini, spread 1½ teaspoons pesto on each baguette slice. Top with a lemon slice and a drizzle of honey. Season with salt.

Roasted Carrot Bruschetta

4 carrots, julienned
¼ cup olive oil
¼ cup maple syrup, plus extra for drizzling
Salt and pepper, to taste
8 (½-inch-thick) slices bread, toasted
½ cup pesto, such as carrot top pesto
1 cup grated or shredded cheese (any variety)

Preheat the oven to 400°F. Line a large rimmed baking sheet with parchment paper.

Put the carrots on the prepared baking sheet. Drizzle them with the olive oil and maple syrup. Season with salt and pepper. Toss the carrots until well coated, then spread them out into a single layer. Roast for 10 to 20 minutes, until tender. Remove the baking sheet from the oven and set aside. Turn on the broiler.

Lay out the toasted bread slices on another baking sheet. Spread 1 tablespoon pesto on each slice and top with 3 to 5 pieces of the roasted carrots. Sprinkle 2 tablespoons cheese on top and broil for 1 to 3 minutes, until the cheese melts. Do not walk away from the broiler—cheese goes from gooey and delicious to burnt in no time flat!

Spicy Pesto Shrimp Bruschetta

½ pound extra large shrimp (26/30 count), peeled, deveined, and cooked (see Note on page 98)
¾ cup pesto, such as Sun-Dried Tomato Pesto (page 30), divided
Juice of 1 lime
⅛ teaspoon cayenne pepper or paprika
Salt and pepper, to taste
8 (½-inch-thick) slices ciabatta bread, toasted
½ cup grated Asiago, divided

Turn on the broiler. Line a large rimmed baking sheet with lightly greased aluminum foil.

In a large bowl, toss the shrimp with ¼ cup of the pesto, the lime juice, and cayenne pepper. Season with salt and pepper.

Place the toasted bread slices on the prepared baking sheet. Spread 1 tablespoon of the remaining pesto on each slice, then place 1 or 2 shrimp on top. Sprinkle each with 1 tablespoon cheese. Broil until the cheese is bubbling, 1 to 3 minutes. Do not walk away from the broiler! Check at 1 minute, for the broiler tends to burn things quickly.

NOTE: If you have any leftover crostini, also known as "little toasts," they make wonderful croutons to be used in a salad or soup.

Appetizers and Small Bites

Pesto adds brightness and personality to common
hors d'oeuvres. Focusing on attractive, easy-to-eat
appetizers and bites done tapas style (more commonly
known as "small plates"), this chapter offers recipes
sure to please a crowd. You may find that your favorite
appetizer can be upgraded to the dinner menu as well.

Silky Pesto Goat Cheese Terrine

MAKES 6 TO 8 SERVINGS

⏱ READY IN 20 MINUTES

1 (5-ounce) log goat cheese, at
   room temperature
2 tablespoons Classic Basil Pesto
   (page 23)
2 tablespoons Sun-Dried Tomato
   Pesto (page 30)
2 tablespoons Roasted Jalapeño–
   Cilantro Pesto (page 30)
Olive oil, for garnish
Salt, to taste
Rustic crackers or vegetable
   sticks, for serving

This recipe was created when Hope's Gardens had only three flavors of pesto–basil, sun-dried tomato, and jalapeño. I was looking for a great way to promote a gift pack and thought our pesto would pair nicely with one of the artisan cheeses at the farmers market. Each layer features a different pesto; when assembled, the flavors meld into a creamy delight. It is one of my favorite mid-afternoon snacks. Feel free to try your own combination of pesto flavors.

Place the log of cheese between two pieces of wax paper. Using a rolling pin, roll out the goat cheese to a thickness of about ¼ inch. Use a 2½-inch round cookie cutter to cut out four circles of cheese.

To assemble the terrine, place one cheese round on a plate and top with the basil pesto. Place another cheese round on top, followed by the sun-dried tomato pesto. Place the third cheese round on top of that and add the jalapeño-cilantro pesto. Top with the last cheese round. Drizzle olive oil over the top and season with salt. Serve with rustic crackers or vegetable sticks.

Cool Cucumber Bites with Shrimp Salad

MAKES 20 SERVINGS

⏱ READY IN 10 MINUTES

1 English cucumber

½ pound small shrimp (50/60 count), peeled, deveined, and cooked (see Note)

¼ cup pesto, such as dill pesto, plus 2 tablespoons for garnish

Grated zest and juice of ½ lemon

2 tablespoons white wine vinegar

2 tablespoons mayonnaise

2 tablespoons chopped celery

Salt and pepper, to taste

These small bites have a cool, crunchy deliciousness to them. They are easy finger foods for both small and large gatherings.

Cut the cucumber crosswise into about 20 (¼-inch-thick) slices. Place the slices on paper towels to absorb any liquid. Chop the poached shrimp. In a large bowl, combine the pesto, lemon zest and juice, vinegar, mayonnaise, and celery. Season with salt and pepper. Add the chopped shrimp and stir well.

To assemble, arrange the cucumber slices on a platter and season them with salt. Top each cucumber slice with 1 teaspoon of the shrimp mixture. Garnish with additional pesto and serve.

NOTE: You can buy cooked shrimp at the grocery store, but you can also poach them yourself. Bring a large pot of water to a boil over medium-high heat, add the raw shrimp (already peeled and deveined), and turn the heat to low. Simmer for about 3 minutes, until the shrimp turn pink. Watch them carefully to make sure they do not overcook and turn tough. Transfer the shrimp to paper towels to absorb any leftover liquid, and let them cool.

Grilled Eggplant Roll-Ups with Spicy Pesto Aioli

MAKES 12 SERVINGS

⏱ READY IN 20 MINUTES

2 large eggplants
1 tablespoon olive oil
Salt and pepper, to taste
½ cup ricotta
¼ cup pesto
½ teaspoon grated lemon zest
½ teaspoon lemon juice
Pinch red pepper flakes
½ cup Spicy Pesto Aioli (page 27)
Parmigiano Reggiano, for garnish

These delicious, creamy appetizer bites melt in your mouth. The eggplant becomes creamy when grilled and absorbs the flavors of the pesto aioli. To get perfect grill marks, make sure the grill pan is very hot and your eggplant is not too thick or too wet. Once you get the hang of rolling the eggplant slices, try it with a zucchini or cucumber.

Warm a grill pan or nonstick skillet over high heat.

Trim the top and bottom off the eggplants. Using a sharp knife, cut each eggplant lengthwise into at least six ¼-inch-thick slices. Brush both sides of the eggplant slices with olive oil and season with salt and pepper. Working in batches, grill the eggplant slices for about 2 minutes per side, until they have grill marks and are slightly softened. Set the eggplant slices aside to cool.

In a small bowl, mix together the ricotta, pesto, lemon zest and juice, and red pepper flakes. Season with salt and pepper and stir to combine.

To assemble the roll-ups, spread 1 tablespoon of the ricotta mixture over each eggplant slice. Starting at the narrow end, roll up the eggplant and secure it with a toothpick. Place each roll, seam side down, on a platter and drizzle with the pesto aioli.

Grate Parmigiano Reggiano over the top to garnish and serve.

Pesto-Stuffed Mushroom Caps

MAKES 16 MUSHROOM CAPS
◷ READY IN 20 MINUTES

16 button mushrooms
1 tablespoon olive oil, plus extra
    for drizzling
Salt and pepper, to taste
¼ cup pesto
¼ cup cream cheese
4 slices Gruyère or Asiago,
    quartered
6 tablespoons breadcrumbs
Hot sauce, for garnish

NOTE: Use a muffin tin as
an alternative to a baking
sheet. It holds the mush-
room caps perfectly.

This retro-inspired finger food is a very easy, last-minute savory hors d'oeuvre to prepare when friends drop by unexpect-
edly. Turn this meat-like substitute into a meal atop a bed of
pasta drizzled with pesto oil. Your friends may never leave!

Preheat the oven 400°F. Line a large rimmed baking sheet
with parchment paper.

Lightly rinse the mushroom caps to dislodge any dirt or sedi-
ment; pat dry. Remove and discard the stems.

Place the mushrooms on the prepared baking sheet. Drizzle
with the tablespoon of olive oil and season with salt and pepper. Toss to evenly coat the mushrooms, then arrange them cap
sides up. Bake for 10 minutes.

While the mushrooms are baking, blend the pesto and cream
cheese together and set aside.

Remove the mushrooms from the oven and flip them over, but
keep the oven on. When they are cool enough to handle, fill
each mushroom cavity with 1½ teaspoons of the pesto mixture.
If the mushrooms have released liquid on the baking sheet,
use a paper towel to absorb as much as you can. Place a piece
of cheese on each mushroom. Top each cap with 1 teaspoon
breadcrumbs.

Drizzle the mushrooms with some olive oil, and season each
with a light pinch of salt and pepper. Place the mushrooms
back in the oven for another 10 minutes, or until the cheese
melts.

Drizzle with hot sauce and serve.

Spicy Jalapeño Guacamole

MAKES 6 SERVINGS

⊙ READY IN 10 MINUTES

2 large or 3 medium ripe avocados, peeled, pitted (pits reserved), and medium diced

1 small Vidalia or red onion, chopped

1 pint cherry tomatoes, halved

¼ cup cilantro leaves

2 garlic cloves, minced

¼ cup Roasted Jalapeño–Cilantro Pesto (page 30)

Juice of 1 lime

Salt and pepper, to taste

1 scallion, white part only, thinly sliced, for garnish

2 teaspoons diced jalapeño, for garnish

Pita chips, for serving

Many years back, I gained a reputation for making killer guacamole that balanced flavor, texture, and color. It found its way onto many party menus at our home. Once we introduced our Hope's Gardens Jalapeño Pesto, I knew our guacamole had met its perfect flavor partner. The sweet and sharp roasted jalapeños melded perfectly into our chunky guacamole. Our favorite way to serve guacamole is with pita chips. I am willing to bet that this dish will be gone in minutes, but if any is left over, it makes a great sandwich spread.

Combine the avocados, onion, tomatoes, cilantro, garlic, pesto, and lime juice in a large bowl. Season with salt and pepper. Toss to mix everything together.

Place the pits in the center, underneath the guacamole, to discourage browning. Garnish with the scallions and jalapeños, and serve with pita chips.

The Devil May Care Eggs

MAKES 12 SERVINGS

⊙ READY IN 20 MINUTES

6 hardboiled eggs (see method on
    page 8), halved lengthwise
2 tablespoons mayonnaise
2 tablespoons pesto
½ teaspoon Dijon mustard
¼ teaspoon white wine vinegar
Salt and pepper, to taste
Paprika or turmeric, for garnish
2 scallions (white parts only),
    thinly sliced, for garnish

Who doesn't like a deviled egg? This classic appetizer is rich and creamy, and with the addition of pesto, you may be able to claim it's "good for you." Always keep your eyes open for pretty deviled egg plates at a reasonable price–I've found many at flea markets and house sales.

Using a sharp knife, halve each egg lengthwise. Remove the yolks and put them in a large bowl. Add the mayonnaise, pesto, mustard, and white wine vinegar. Season with salt and pepper and mash everything together. Transfer the mixture to a plastic zip-top bag. Cut the tip off one corner of the bag. Pipe the mixture into the egg whites.

Sprinkle with paprika and garnish with the scallion slices. Serve.

Creamy Pesto Hummus with Cut Vegetables

MAKES 12 SERVINGS

⏱ **READY IN 15 MINUTES**

1 (15.5-ounce) can cannellini beans, rinsed and drained

2 tablespoons tahini

1 garlic clove

¼ teaspoon grated lemon zest, plus extra for garnish

2½ tablespoons lemon juice

¼ teaspoon salt

¼ teaspoon pepper

½ cup olive oil, plus extra for garnish

½ cup pesto

Chopped herbs, such as chives, cilantro, and/or parsley, for garnish

Assorted cut-up vegetables, such as carrots, radishes, celery, bell peppers, and cucumbers, for serving

NOTE: Are you familiar with tahini? Tahini is a paste from the eastern Mediterranean region made from sesame seeds that have been hulled (the outer covering has been removed) and toasted.

When our pesto business started to take off, we wanted to offer our customers something new, so we started making hummus. One day, it became clear that combining our hummus with the delicious flavors of our pesto made perfect sense. That's how this creamy delicious hummus was born. I hope it will become one of your favorite go-to spreads.

In a food processor, combine the beans, tahini, garlic, lemon zest and juice, salt, and pepper. Pour the olive oil slowly through the feed tube and begin blending. Scrape down the sides with a rubber spatula. Add the pesto and more olive oil, lemon juice, or water if the mixture seems dry.

Transfer the hummus to a bowl and garnish with a drizzle of olive oil, lemon zest, and the chopped herbs. Surround with the vegetables and serve.

Pesto-Drizzled Grilled Chicken Satay

MAKES 16 SKEWERS

READY IN 20 MINUTES

¼ cup pesto, such as Thai-inspired
  pesto
¼ cup rice wine vinegar
¼ cup lime juice
1 teaspoon grated fresh ginger
Salt and pepper, to taste
1 pound boneless, skinless chicken
  tenderloins or breasts, cut
  lengthwise into 16 thin slices
¼ cup crushed peanuts or cashews,
  for garnish

My family and I are crazy for Thai food. When we go out to a restaurant, one of our favorite appetizers is chicken satay with peanut sauce. I always like to recreate restaurant dishes at home, and of course, pesto is always a component of our home dishes. To tie in with the Thai influence (how is that for a pun!), try creating a Thai-inspired pesto with peanuts and cilantro. If you are looking for a different protein, substitute thin slices of steak for the chicken.

Soak 16 (8-inch) wooden skewers in water for 15 minutes. Meanwhile, mix together the pesto, vinegar, lime juice, and ginger. Season with salt and pepper.

Put the chicken in a bowl and pour in half of the vinaigrette; toss to coat well. Mix to combine. Thread one slice of chicken onto each wooden skewer.

Lightly grease a grill pan and set it over medium-high heat. Place the skewers on it and cook for 2 to 3 minutes per side. Remember, to get perfect grill marks, you need a very hot grill pan and chicken breasts that are not too thick.

To serve, arrange the grilled skewers around the perimeter of a platter. Sprinkle with the crushed nuts. Pour the remaining vinaigrette into a bowl and place it in the center for dipping.

Skewered Hors d'Oeuvres Platter

MAKES 12 SERVINGS (6 SKEWERS EACH)

⊘ READY IN 30 MINUTES

Get your party started in style with these skewered hors d'oeuvres that are easy for grabbing and walking around a party—no plates or napkins necessary. If you end up with leftovers, they can easily be added to a salad or a wrap. The options are limitless.

Caprese Skewers

1 pint multicolored cherry tomatoes
1 (8-ounce) container mini fresh mozzarella
  balls (ciliegine), drained
24 basil leaves
¼ cup pesto
2 tablespoons balsamic vinegar
2 tablespoons olive oil

Thread 1 tomato, 1 mozzarella ball, and 1 basil leaf on each of 24 (8-inch) wooden skewers. Mix the pesto, vinegar, and olive oil together. Drizzle a small amount over each skewer.

Shrimp Skewers

4 tablespoons Compound Pesto Butter
  (any flavor; page 29)
1 pound jumbo shrimp (21/25 count), peeled,
  deveined, and cooked (see page 98)

Warm the compound pesto butter in a saucepan for a minute. Add the cooked shrimp and toss to coat. Thread the shrimp lengthwise on each of 24 (8-inch) wooden skewers.

Tortellini Skewers

1 pound fresh or dried tortellini,
  any filling you like
¼ cup pesto
2 tablespoons olive oil
Salt and pepper, to taste
1 large fresh mozzarella ball, cut into
  24 (½-inch) cubes
24 small pitted green olives

Bring a large pot of salted water to a boil. Add the tortellini and cook according to package instructions. Drain the tortellini and return them to the pot. Add the pesto and olive oil, season with salt and pepper, and mix well. Thread each of 24 (8-inch) wooden skewers with one tortellini, one cube of mozzarella, and one olive. If there is any pesto oil left in the pot, drizzle it over the prepared skewers.

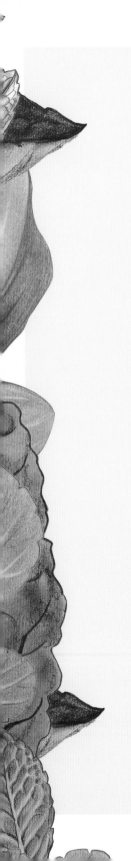

Soups

Infusing dimension and fragrance, pesto can be
used as a base for soups and stews, or it can be
swirled in as a finishing touch. Dive in and discover
soups to warm your bones on a freezing day or cool
you down in the thick heat of summer.

Gazpacho Shooters with Chilled Pesto Cubes

MAKES 4 SERVINGS
○ READY IN 15 MINUTES

3 thick slices day-old bread
3 medium tomatoes, chopped
1 English cucumber, chopped, with
   ¼ cup reserved for garnish
2 garlic cloves
2 multicolored bell peppers,
   seeded and chopped, with ¼ cup
   reserved for garnish
1 medium red onion, chopped, with
   ¼ cup reserved for garnish
1 small jalapeño, seeded and
   chopped
1 tablespoon grated lime zest
¼ cup lime juice
¼ cup cilantro leaves
¼ cup white wine vinegar
¼ cup olive oil
Salt and pepper, to taste
4 frozen pesto cubes (see page 20),
   or more as desired

NOTE: My little secret for getting perfectly equal-size dice for garnish is to use a vegetable dicer/chopper/slicer with different size inserts and a container for storage. It makes this step quick and easy with no mess. For a twist on this classic gazpacho, try substituting watermelon or cantaloupe for the tomatoes.

Pesto cubes are a great way to add extra flavor to this smooth gazpacho recipe. I always have a mini ice cube tray filled with pesto ready to go in the freezer. If you prefer a chunky gazpacho, adjust the blender time to get the texture you desire.

Briefly soak the bread in a bowl of water. Remove the bread from the water, squeeze out as much liquid as possible, and transfer it to a food processor or blender. Add the tomatoes, cucumber, garlic, bell peppers, onion, jalapeño, lime zest and juice, cilantro, vinegar, and oil. Season with salt and pepper and blend until smooth.

Pour the gazpacho into four shooters or tall glasses, add a pesto cube to each, and top with the reserved cucumber, bell pepper, and onion. Serve.

Pesto Minestrone for All Seasons

MAKES 6 SERVINGS
⊙ READY IN 30 MINUTES

5 tablespoons olive oil, divided
1 medium carrot, diced
1 celery rib, diced
1 small shallot, thinly sliced
½ cup shelled edamame
¼ cup corn kernels
1 medium white potato, diced
5 ounces sugar snap peas,
    chopped
8 cups water
2 scallions, sliced into ½-inch
    pieces
1 cup cooked orzo
1 (15.5-ounce) can white beans,
    such as great Northern or
    cannellini, rinsed and drained
Salt and pepper, to taste
¼ cup parsley
1 cup arugula
Juice of ½ lemon
¼ cup pesto
½ cup mixed herbs, such as thyme,
    mint, dill, and/or chives, for
    garnish
Grated parmesan, for garnish

Minestrone is a seasonal Italian vegetable soup loaded with the bounty from the garden. Adding fiber- and protein-rich beans will make this a filling, comforting, and satisfying meal in one bowl. As the seasons change, so can the soup's primary ingredients and the pesto you use. Pea or mint pesto would be ideal for springtime, while a kale or sun-dried tomato pesto would be perfect for winter.

Heat 1 tablespoon of the olive oil in a Dutch oven over medium-high heat. Add the carrot, celery, and shallot. Stir and cook for 3 minutes. Add the edamame, corn kernels, potato, and sugar snap peas. Stir and cook for another 3 minutes. Add the water, and cook for 5 minutes to create your own vegetable broth.

Add the scallions, orzo, and white beans. Season with salt and pepper and cover. Reduce the heat to low and simmer for 10 minutes to let the flavors combine.

Right before serving, add the parsley, arugula, and lemon juice to brighten the soup. Separately, combine the pesto and remaining 4 tablespoons olive oil. When ready to serve, ladle the soup into individual bowls and drizzle with the pesto oil. Garnish with the mixed herbs and grated cheese.

NOTE: Try using some of the leftover crostini from page 91 as a giant crouton to round out each bowl.

Chicken Pesto Noodle Soup

MAKES 8 SERVINGS

⏱ READY IN 60 MINUTES

1 (2-pound) rotisserie chicken

8 cups water

1 small onion, diced

2 carrots, diced

2 celery stalks with leaves, diced

1 medium potato, diced

2 garlic cloves, minced

Salt and pepper, to taste

¾ cup broken thin egg noodles or capellini

¼ cup mixed herbs, such as dill, parsley, and/or basil leaves

1 cup pesto

Grated parmesan, for garnish

NOTE: The flavors will develop the longer the soup cooks. The longer it sits, the more extra liquid you may have to add, as the noodles tend to soak up the broth.

Nothing soothes a cold like chicken noodle soup. Add a dollop of Classic Basil Pesto (page 23) or dill or parsley pesto, and begin benefiting from these herbs' immune-boosting properties so you can start feeling better immediately!

Put the chicken in a large Dutch oven and pour in the water. Bring to a boil over medium-high heat and then lower the heat to medium. Add all the vegetables and stir. Season with salt and pepper. Cover, reduce the heat to low, and simmer for 30 minutes.

Transfer the chicken to a cutting board and separate the meat from the bones. Shred the white meat and return it to the pot. Reserve the dark meat for a future use; discard the skin and bones. Cover the pot and simmer the soup, still over low heat, for another 30 minutes.

Bring a small pot of salted water to a boil over medium-high heat and cook the noodles until al dente. Drain and add the noodles to the soup. Just before serving, add the herbs. Ladle the soup into bowls. Swirl 1 tablespoon or more of pesto into each bowl, garnish with grated parmesan, and serve.

Pesto Ramen Bowl

MAKES 4 SERVINGS

⏱ READY IN 20 MINUTES

4 cups vegetable broth (see method on page 8) or chicken broth
1 tablespoon soy sauce
1 scallion, thinly sliced, white and green parts separated
1 (½-inch) piece fresh ginger, grated
1 tablespoon olive oil
1 small onion, thinly sliced
2 large mushrooms (any variety), thinly sliced
1 bell pepper (any color), seeded and thinly sliced
4 brussels sprouts, thinly sliced
10 ounces ramen noodles
1 carrot, julienned or thinly shaved
1 endive, thinly sliced
2 hardboiled eggs (see method on page 8), halved lengthwise
Roasted seaweed sheets, torn, for garnish
4 tablespoons pesto

A bowl of ramen noodles is one of the quickest and easiest comfort foods you can make. Start with a great broth and the freshest noodles you can find. Don't be put off by this long list of ingredients. Most of this recipe can be prepared in advance, and your ramen bowl can come together in minutes.

In a medium saucepan, warm the broth over medium heat. Add the soy sauce, scallion whites, and ginger. Simmer for 10 minutes to deepen the flavor.

Heat the oil in a nonstick skillet over medium-high heat. Add the onion and cook, stirring frequently, until the onion caramelizes and turns golden, 5 to 7 minutes. Transfer to a small bowl and set aside. Add the mushrooms and cook, stirring frequently, for 3 minutes. Transfer to a small bowl and set aside. Add the bell pepper and cook, stirring frequently, for 3 minutes. Transfer to a small bowl and set aside. Add the brussels sprouts and cook, stirring frequently, for 3 minutes. Transfer to a small bowl and set aside.

Bring a large pot of water to a boil over medium-high heat. Add the ramen noodles and cook until tender, about 3 minutes. Transfer the noodles to a colander; drain and rinse well.

To assemble, use kitchen tongs to divide the noodles among four large bowls. Ladle the hot broth over the noodles. For visual interest, add small amounts of the onion, mushrooms, bell pepper, brussels sprouts, carrot, endive, and egg halves in a circular pattern. Then, top each bowl with a few pieces of torn seaweed, 1 tablespoon pesto, and the scallion greens for garnish.

TRI-COLOR ROASTED VEGGIE SOUP BAR
page 122

Roasted Carrot and Butternut Squash Soup

Roasted Broccoli Potato Soup

Roasted Beet and Bean Soup

Tri-Color Roasted Veggie Soup Bar

MAKES 12 SERVINGS

⏱ READY IN 1½ TO 2 HOURS

Pictured on previous page

This is a great fall or wintertime party idea. These three soups, accessorized with your favorite pestos, will make your guests feel cozy and warm. Set out all the soups and create a toppings bar with dishes of shredded cheeses, pestos, croutons, and sour cream or Greek yogurt. Then, have your guests build their own bowls of unique flavor combinations. Remember to keep the size of your vegetables consistent so that they cook evenly and get done at the same time. To avoid a logistical nightmare, try making the soups a day in advance and reheating the day of the party. If your oven will accommodate, roast the vegetables for all three soups at one time. Remember to keep your soups warm when serving; try using slow cookers, tabletop burners, warming trays, chafers, or the stovetop. The main thing is to bring people together for good times and good food!

Roasted Carrot and Butternut Squash Soup

2 carrots, chopped
1 small butternut squash, peeled, seeded, and cubed
1 medium sweet onion, chopped
1 teaspoon minced fresh ginger
1 tablespoon olive oil
1 tablespoon maple syrup
Salt and pepper, to taste
4 cups vegetable broth (see method on page 8) or chicken broth
½ cup pesto, such as carrot top pesto, for garnish

Preheat the oven to 400°F. Line a large rimmed baking sheet with parchment paper.

In a bowl, toss together the carrots, squash, onion, ginger, olive oil, and maple syrup. Season with salt and pepper. Transfer the vegetable mixture to the prepared baking sheet. Roast for 30 minutes, or until the vegetables are tender and golden.

While the vegetables are roasting, warm the broth in a large saucepan over medium-low heat. Add the roasted vegetables to the broth. If you have an immersion blender, use it to create a smooth soup. If not, a regular blender will get the job done in batches—just make sure to remove the center from the blender lid and place a dish towel over the hole to allow the steam to escape; otherwise, the lid can blow off!

When ready to serve, have your guests ladle the soup into bowls, swirl in a spoonful of pesto, and add toppings.

Roasted Broccoli Potato Soup

1 large head broccoli, cut into florets, stem reserved for pesto
6 small white potatoes, quartered
2 garlic cloves, chopped
1 tablespoon olive oil
Salt and pepper, to taste
4 cups vegetable broth (see method on page 8) or chicken broth
½ cup pesto, such as broccoli stem pesto, for garnish

Preheat the oven to 400°F. Line a large rimmed baking sheet with parchment paper.

In a bowl, toss together the broccoli florets, potatoes, garlic, and olive oil. Season with salt and pepper. Transfer the vegetable mixture to the prepared baking sheet. Roast for 30 minutes, or until the vegetables are tender and slightly charred.

While the vegetables are roasting, warm the broth in a large saucepan over medium-low heat. Add the roasted vegetables to the broth. If you have an immersion blender, use it to create a smooth soup. If not, a regular blender will get the job done in batches—just make sure to remove the center from the blender lid and place a dish towel over the hole to allow the steam to escape; otherwise, the lid can blow off!

When ready to serve, have your guests ladle the soup into bowls, swirl in a spoonful of pesto, and add toppings.

Roasted Beet and Bean Soup

1 large beet
1 large red onion, chopped
1 garlic clove, chopped
1 tablespoon olive oil
Salt and pepper, to taste
4 cups vegetable broth (see method on
  page 8) or chicken broth
1 (15.5-ounce) can white beans, such as great
  Northern or cannellini, drained and rinsed
½ cup pesto, such as beet greens pesto, for
  garnish

Preheat the oven to 400°F. Line a large rimmed baking sheet with parchment paper.

Wearing gloves to avoid staining your hands, peel the beet using a vegetable peeler. Chop the beet into medium pieces and transfer to a bowl. Add the red onion, garlic, and olive oil and toss to combine. Season with salt and pepper. Transfer the beet mixture to the prepared baking sheet. Roast for 30 minutes, or until the beet has softened.

While the vegetables are roasting, warm the broth in a large saucepan over medium-low heat. Add the white beans and roasted beet mixture to the broth. If you have an immersion blender, use it to create a smooth soup. If not, a regular blender will get the job done in batches—just make sure to remove the center from the blender lid and place a dish towel over the hole to allow the steam to escape; otherwise, the lid can blow off!

When ready to serve, have your guests ladle the soup into bowls, swirl in a spoonful of pesto, and add toppings.

NOTE: There is no added cream or butter in any of these recipes. The sweetness comes from the caramelization of the vegetables. If you prefer a creamier soup, add plain Greek yogurt before blending.

Pesto Pork Wonton Soup

MAKES 6 SERVINGS

⏱ READY IN 30 MINUTES

8 ounces pork sausage, casings removed

½ cup finely minced cabbage

1 tablespoon minced fresh ginger

1 tablespoon minced garlic

1 tablespoon minced shallot

2 scallions, thinly sliced, white and green parts separated

1 teaspoon soy sauce

1 tablespoon pesto

¼ cup water

24 square wonton wrappers

8 cups vegetable broth (see method on page 8) or chicken broth

2 tablespoons soy sauce

1 teaspoon toasted sesame oil

NOTE: The wontons can be prepared in advance and frozen in a zip-top bag for up to 1 month.

These little bundles of meat steam in the warm broth. When you bite into one, you experience an explosion of rich flavors and textures.

Combine the pork, cabbage, ginger, garlic, shallot, scallion whites, soy sauce, pesto, and water in a large bowl. Toss to mix well.

Fill a small bowl with water. Place one wonton wrapper on a clean, dry work surface. Dip your finger in the water and gently dampen the outer edge of the wrapper. Be careful not to use too much water, as your wrappers will become soggy quickly. Place a rounded 1½ teaspoon of the meat filling in the center of the wrapper and fold it over diagonally into a triangle, pressing on the edges to create a seal. Then, fold the two outer corners into the center so that they overlap; press to seal. Transfer the wonton to a plate and cover with a damp paper towel to prevent it from drying out. Repeat this process with the remaining wrappers and filling. Refrigerate the wontons until ready to cook.

In a large stockpot, bring the broth, soy sauce, sesame oil, and scallion greens to a boil over medium-high heat. Lower the heat to medium-low and carefully add the wontons. Simmer for 5 minutes, or until the pork is cooked through. The wontons will float to the surface of the broth when they are ready.

Ladle the broth and wontons into bowls and serve.

Vegetables

Fresh, in-season vegetables are at the heart of Hope's Gardens. In this chapter, you will find recipes for mouthwatering vegetable-based salads, sides, and mains that you can vary every time you select another flavor of pesto. In addition, find ways to show off a vegetable with a short season, such as summer tomatoes, spring asparagus, or fall mushrooms. Look to lift your meal by adding a homemade dressing (see pages 26 to 27) or a drizzle of pesto-infused oil. With a little planning, you'll be able to showcase a modern, irresistible meal.

Heartbeet Salad with Orange–Honey Mustard Vinaigrette

MAKES 4 SERVINGS
⏱ READY IN 75 MINUTES

2 medium beets
2 tablespoons water
¼ cup pesto
¼ cup crumbled goat cheese,
  at room temperature
1 orange, peeled and thinly sliced
  crosswise
Salt and pepper, to taste
Orange-Honey Mustard
  Vinaigrette (recipe follows),
  for drizzling
¼ cup crushed pistachios,
  for garnish

NOTE: This recipe works great with standard beets and navel oranges (pictured on the following pages), but you can also mix things up with different varieties. One of my favorite combinations is a candy cane beet with a cara cara orange (pictured at left).

I first made this dish for my husband, Dave, one Valentine's Day long ago. We had beautiful beets growing in our garden, and with the help of a heart-shaped cookie cutter, this dish got its name.

Preheat the oven to 400°F.

Place the beets on a sheet of aluminum foil and add the water. Fold up the foil to enclose the beets in a tight packet. Place the packet on a small baking sheet and roast for 45 to 60 minutes, until the beets are soft and easily pierced with the tip of a knife.

Combine the pesto and the softened goat cheese and set the mixture aside.

When the beets are done, remove them from the oven, let them cool, and then remove their outer skin by rubbing it off. Wear rubber gloves to avoid staining your hands. Cut each one crosswise into three or four even slices.

Using a heart-shaped cookie cutter, cut through each beet slice. (Save the beet ends to use in a salad or a wrap.) To assemble the salad, place three orange slices on each plate. Top with one or two heartbeets, depending on the size of your cookie cutter. Season with salt and pepper. Add 1 tablespoon of the pesto mixture and a drizzle of the vinaigrette on top of each serving. Garnish with the crushed nuts and serve.

Orange-Honey Mustard Vinaigrette

MAKES ¾ CUP

¼ cup olive oil
¼ cup white wine vinegar
¼ cup orange juice
1 tablespoon honey mustard

Combine all the ingredients in a lidded jar. Shake well. Serve immediately or store in the refrigerator for up to 2 weeks.

**HEARTBEET SALAD WITH
ORANGE–HONEY MUSTARD
VINAIGRETTE** *page 129*

Seasonal Salads with Pesto Dressings and Homemade Croutons

MAKES 8 SERVINGS
⏱ READY IN 60 MINUTES

I grew up eating salads every day. My mother was a great cook and would begin the day pulling out the vegetable bin and cutting up a big, beautiful salad. This has become a lifelong habit for just about every meal I prepare. Salads are always better when you choose seasonal ingredients. During the summer months, browse your local farmers market to find the freshest lettuce varieties. In the winter, the best lettuces you can find will be hardy and dark. With some extra add-ins, such as hardboiled eggs or other protein, roasted squash, grains, or rice, this salad can function as an entrée or a perfect side dish. Look to the recommendations below and mix and match to suit your preferences!

Summer Greens with Buttermilk Pesto Dressing

6 cups chopped summer greens, such as butterhead, baby romaine, baby arugula, and/or radicchio
½ cup quartered radishes, such as breakfast, watermelon, daikon, and Easter egg
1 large endive, thinly sliced on the diagonal
½ medium fennel bulb, thinly sliced
1 small jicama, julienned
1 cup Homemade Croutons (recipe follows)
½ cup Buttermilk Pesto Dressing (page 27)

Combine the greens, radishes, endive, fennel, and jicama in a wide, shallow bowl ideal for tossing. Pour in the dressing and toss well with either your hands or wooden salad spoons. Top with the croutons and serve.

Winter Greens with Kale Pesto Dressing

6 cups chopped winter greens, such as kale, mustard greens, collards, Swiss chard, arugula, spinach, mâche, and/or turnip greens
½ cup Kale Pesto Dressing (page 27)
1 cup Homemade Croutons (recipe follows)
4 hardboiled eggs (see method on page 8), halved lengthwise

Put the greens in a wide, shallow bowl ideal for tossing. Pour in the dressing and toss well with either your hands or wooden salad spoons. Top with the croutons and eggs. Serve.

Homemade Croutons

MAKES 1 CUP

3 slices day-old bread
1 tablespoon olive oil
Salt and pepper, to taste

Preheat the oven to 325°F. Line a large rimmed baking sheet with parchment paper or lightly greased aluminum foil.

Cut the bread into 1-inch cubes. In a bowl, toss the cubes with the olive oil and season with salt and pepper. Place in a single layer on the prepared baking sheet and bake for 10 minutes, until the croutons are toasted and golden. Store any leftover croutons in a sealed container for a few days.

SALAD TIPS

You're likely familiar with the wall of greens available at most grocery stores. But did you know that different types of greens contribute different qualities to your salad? Knowing the difference will help you build better, more flavorful salads. According to *New York Times* food writer Julia Moskin, there are four general categories of greens:

Soft greens and herbs, such as baby lettuce and spinach, spring mix, and butterhead lettuce. These are usually sweet, with pale or light green leaves, and wilt easily. You'll want to use these greens soon after purchasing them and try not to overwhelm them with too much dressing. The whole leaves also make wonderful lettuce wraps, such as our Pesto Sausage Lettuce Wraps (page 189), or try topping them with roasted pears and feta.

All-purpose greens, such as romaine, iceberg lettuce, and baby arugula. These greens are mild and crisper than soft greens. As their name suggests, they are perfect as the base for everyday salads, and they add a satisfying crunch. Classics such as a Caesar salad or a wedge salad drenched in blue cheese dressing are often associated with these greens. I like to top a mound of these chopped greens with an Asian-inspired dressing, toasted almonds, slivered carrots, and grilled chicken for an entrée.

Sturdy greens, such as chard, kale, and spinach. These greens are dark in color with thick leaves that don't wilt easily. They also tend to have thick, woody stems, which you may need to remove before eating (save them for pesto!). These greens can generally be stored in the coldest part of your refrigerator for two or three days. I like to add these greens to my salad for a healthy dose of vitamins A and C and iron. Try them in a warm wilted salad with mushrooms and bacon bits or make our Ultimate Veggie Collard Wraps (page 137)–you can easily substitute a beautiful chard leaf for the collard.

Peppery greens, such as arugula, endive, and watercress. These greens pack a powerful punch of flavor. They can be bitter, with assertive mustard and pepper notes. These greens can come on a bit strong on their own for some palates, but try mixing them into your salad for a bit more bite. I love to top these spicy greens with thinly sliced radishes and crumbled goat cheese. They also work nicely mixed into a grain or pasta salad.

I like to try to use all four types of greens in each salad I make, then dress it up with a delicious vinaigrette and some crunch. Croutons (see the recipe on this page) are the obvious choice, but you may want to try different textural toppings. My favorites are slivered or chopped toasted nuts; seeds; crispy, pickled, or caramelized onions and shallots; roasted chickpeas; dried fruits; crumbled cheese; and sliced avocado. Select one or two at a time for the salad, so as to not overwhelm and confuse your taste buds.

Use this as a reference to create explosive salads. By no means do you need to stick to one category. Mix and match, and look for what is in season and local to your home.

Caprese Salad with Pesto Vinaigrette

MAKES 2 ENTRÉE SERVINGS OR 4 SIDE DISH SERVINGS
⏱ READY IN 10 MINUTES

4 cups cherry tomatoes
4 cups fresh mini mozzarella balls
  (ciliegine)
1 cup gently torn fresh basil leaves
½ cup Classic Pesto Vinaigrette
  (page 26)

NOTE: For a twist, try swapping
ripe, sweet strawberries for the
tomatoes when they are in season!
When you roughly chop the tomatoes and mozzarella into smaller
pieces, this recipe becomes the
perfect topping for cooked pasta
or bruschetta.

One summer when our garden was overflowing with tomatoes,
I created this easy and fresh-tasting dish based on the classic
Southern Italian caprese. On a hot day, cool down by serving it
either as a side dish or as a light meal with a fresh baguette. I
like to use bite-size cherry tomatoes in this recipe because they
complement the small mozzarella balls (known as *ciliegine*, which
means "cherry" in Italian), but you can use any type you wish.

Toss the tomatoes, mozzarella, and basil leaves together in a
large bowl. Add the vinaigrette. Toss again and serve.

Ultimate Veggie Collard Wraps

MAKES 2 SERVINGS
⏱ READY IN 40 MINUTES

2 cups (½-inch) vegetable cubes,
  such as eggplant, zucchini,
  carrot, bell pepper, and/or beet
1 tablespoon olive oil
Salt and pepper, to taste
2 large collard green leaves
4 tablespoons Creamy Pesto
  Hummus (page 106)
4 tablespoons cooked quinoa
2 radishes, thinly sliced

A collard green leaf makes a great wrap alternative to a flour tortilla, and it's high in vitamins to boot. Prepare all your ingredients in advance, and then you are only minutes away from a very filling and satisfying lunch or dinner. Leftover quinoa from the Pesto Quinoa-Stuffed Roasted Red Peppers (page 146) works perfectly.

Preheat the oven to 400°F. Line a large rimmed baking sheet with parchment paper or lightly greased aluminum foil.

In a bowl, toss the vegetables with the oil. Season with salt and pepper. Transfer the vegetables to the prepared baking sheet. Roast for 30 minutes, or until the vegetables are soft and golden.

Rinse and dry the collard green leaves, then carefully trim away as much of the center spines as possible while keeping the leaves intact. Lay the collard green leaves flat. Spread 2 tablespoons of the pesto hummus down the center of each leaf. Add 2 tablespoons of the quinoa and 1 cup of the roasted vegetables. Place a few overlapping radish slices on each. Tuck in both ends of the collard leaf and roll. Serve as is or cut each wrap diagonally across the center.

Prosciutto-Wrapped Asparagus Spears

MAKES 4 SIDE DISH SERVINGS OR 12 APPETIZER SERVINGS
⏱ READY IN 30 MINUTES

½ cup pesto
½ cup cream cheese, at room
   temperature
12 slices prosciutto
12 asparagus spears, ends trimmed

This recipe does double duty. You can serve it as either a very elegant side dish or a great appetizer. If you are using it as a side, two or three spears alongside your main dish are perfect. Try it with Bacon-Wrapped Pesto-Glazed Pork Tenderloin (page 186). If your asparagus is very thin, double the count and use two per wrap.

Preheat the oven to 400°F. Line a large rimmed baking sheet with parchment paper or lightly greased aluminum foil.

Mix together the pesto and cream cheese. Place the prosciutto slices on a clean work surface. Spread 1 tablespoon of the pesto mixture on top of each slice. Place one asparagus spear at a slight diagonal at one end of a prosciutto slice. Roll up the asparagus tightly in the prosciutto and place it, seam side down, on the baking sheet. Repeat this process with the remaining asparagus.

Roast for 15 minutes, until the prosciutto is crisp and the asparagus are tender. Serve.

"Always Make Extra" Potatoes with Savory Pesto Butter

MAKES 4 SERVINGS

⏱ READY IN 45 MINUTES

1 pound potatoes (fingerling, red, or white), quartered or cut into ½- to 1-inch cubes
4 tablespoons Compound Pesto Butter (page 29), cut into small pieces
Salt and pepper, to taste

This dish always hits the spot. I prepare more than needed so that I can create something different, like a potato hash or wraps, the next day. No matter what size potatoes you start with, make sure they are all cut to a consistent size so they cook evenly in the oven. The result is a crispy, caramelized, buttery delight. Try these potatoes alongside Dave's Pesto-Glazed New York Strip Steak (page 178)!

Preheat the oven to 400°F. Line a large rimmed baking sheet with lightly greased aluminum foil or grease an oval gratin dish with cooking oil spray.

Spread out the potatoes on the prepared baking sheet. Dot the small pieces of pesto butter evenly over the potatoes. Season with salt and pepper.

Roast for 30 to 45 minutes, until the potatoes are crispy and golden.

Cubed Butternut Squash over Pesto Zucchini Noodles

MAKES 2 TO 4 SERVINGS
⏱ READY IN 45 MINUTES

1 large or 2 medium butternut squash, peeled, seeded, and cut into ½-inch cubes
1 tablespoon olive oil
Salt and pepper, to taste
1 pound zucchini noodles, from 3-4 medium zucchinis (see method on page 9)
¼ cup pesto
¼ cup crumbled feta, for garnish
1 cup crushed candied nuts, for garnish

NOTE: Try a "recipe flip" by using butternut squash noodles and roasted zucchini cubes.

I began to spiralize vegetable noodles when I started Weight Watchers. Being in the food world and spending every weekend selling pesto at the Peachtree Road Farmers Market in Atlanta, I quickly gained extra weight. Replacing pasta with vegetable noodles is a great solution and helped me lose close to 20 pounds. This dish can also be prepared without cooking the zucchini noodles for a fresh, raw summer version. I like to use sweet and spicy candied pecans, which add zing to every mouthful.

Preheat the oven to 400°F. Line a large rimmed baking sheet with parchment paper or lightly greased aluminum foil.

Put the squash on the prepared baking sheet, drizzle with the oil, and season with salt and pepper. Roast for 20 to 30 minutes, until the squash is golden.

Place a nonstick skillet over medium-high heat. If the zucchini noodles are extremely long, cut them to a more manageable length, then add them to the skillet. Add the pesto and cook until the zucchini noodles are slightly softened, 3 to 5 minutes.

Divide the pesto zucchini noodles among two or four plates or bowls. Divide the butternut squash cubes among the servings. Garnish with the cheese and nuts. Serve.

Butternut Squash Spaghetti

MAKES 4 SERVINGS
◷ READY IN 20 MINUTES

1 pound butternut squash noodles, from 1 medium to large squash (see method on page 9)
1 tablespoon water
½ cup pancetta cubes or bacon bits
1 cup fresh or rehydrated dried figs or dates, halved or quartered
¼ cup pesto, such as Kale Pesto (page 31)
1 tablespoon olive oil, for drizzling
½ cup crumbled goat cheese or blue cheese
Salt and pepper, to taste

If you are watching your calorie intake, butternut squash is another vegetable you can use in place of pasta for a healthy makeover. It results in an extremely tasty and satisfying meal. If you don't have a spiralizer, you can likely find squash noodles in the produce department of your grocery store. The caramelized figs add a wonderful sweetness to this dish. When they are not in season, replace them with dates. Everything can be done in one large sauté pan, or even a wok, to minimize the cleanup.

Place a large sauté pan or wok over medium-high heat. If the butternut squash noodles are extremely long, cut them to a more manageable length; add them to the pan, along with the water. Cover and let the noodles steam until they have softened, about 5 minutes. Add more water if necessary. Transfer the noodles to a large bowl and set aside.

Add the pancetta cubes to the pan and cook until slightly crisp, about 5 minutes. Transfer to a small bowl and set aside. Add the figs to the pan and cook for several minutes, until they are slightly soft, caramelized, and golden. Transfer to the bowl with the pancetta and set aside.

Return the butternut squash noodles to the pan, along with the pesto. Drizzle the noodles with the oil. Return the figs and pancetta to the pan and sprinkle with the crumbled cheese until it begins to melt. Season with salt and pepper. Gently toss, then serve.

Leaning Eggplant Towers

MAKES 2 ENTRÉE SERVINGS OR 4 FIRST COURSE SERVINGS

⊙ READY IN 75 MINUTES

2 tablespoons olive oil

1 large or 2 medium eggplants, sliced crosswise into a total of 8 (½-inch-thick) medallions

Salt and pepper, to taste

2 tomatoes, sliced crosswise into 8 (½-inch-thick) medallions

1 large white or red onion, sliced crosswise into 8 (½-inch-thick) medallions

1 (1-pound) mozzarella ball, sliced crosswise into 8 (½-inch-thick) medallions

½ cup pesto

2 cups quartered cherry tomatoes

4 ounces capellini

My husband, Dave, has had great success growing different varieties of eggplant in our garden. This recipe is a wonderful reinvention of classic eggplant parmesan, although ours involves no frying, which translates to great flavor and fewer calories–win-win! If you are using this recipe as a main course, try making a double-stacked tower. Another way to serve this is on ciabatta bread for a sandwich on the go.

Preheat the oven to 350°F. Line a large rimmed baking sheet with parchment paper and lightly grease a 9 × 13-inch oval gratin or baking dish. Set both aside.

Brush the olive oil on both sides of each eggplant slice. Season with salt and pepper. Spread out the eggplant slices in a single layer on the prepared baking sheet. Bake for 15 minutes, flip the slices, and continue baking for another 15 minutes. Remove the eggplant from the oven, but keep the oven on.

Transfer the eggplant slices to the prepared gratin dish. On each one, stack a tomato slice, onion slice, and mozzarella slice; you will have 8 individual stacks. Top each stack with 2 teaspoons pesto. Season with salt and pepper. Add the cherry tomatoes to the gratin dish, around the stacks.

Bake for 30 minutes, or until the cheese is bubbling and the towers are slightly soft.

While the towers bake, bring a large pot of water to a boil over medium-high heat. Add the capellini and cook until al dente. Reserve 1 cup of pasta water to use just in case your cooked pasta needs some hydration, then drain the noodles.

Divide the capellini among two or four plates and place one or two eggplant towers on each. Spoon the cherry tomatoes and juice from the baking dish over the eggplant stacks and pasta. Serve.

Pesto Quinoa–Stuffed Roasted Red Peppers

MAKES 4 SERVINGS
⊘ READY IN 40 MINUTES

4 red bell peppers
Salt and pepper, to taste
1 cup quinoa, rinsed
1½ cups vegetable broth (see
    method on page 8), chicken
    broth, or water
¼ cup pesto
Olive oil, for drizzling

NOTE: If you have leftover pesto quinoa, use it to make Ultimate Veggie Collard Wraps (page 137) for lunch the following day.

Dave always liked to experiment in the garden, his "laboratory." He grew many varieties of peppers–jalapeños, bananas, habaneros, and bell peppers, one of our favorites. This dish is inspired by our love of this vegetable and quinoa. Quinoa, filling and satisfying, is a wonderful, healthy seed (often mistaken for a grain) to add as a companion to any meal. Try serving with Oven-Roasted Pesto-Glazed Salmon (see page 170). If you are not a quinoa lover, try using wild rice instead.

Preheat the oven to 400°F. Line a medium baking sheet with parchment paper or lightly greased aluminum foil.

Cut the tops off the peppers and set them aside. Remove and discard the seeds and ribs, being careful not to break through or crack the bell peppers. Season the insides of the peppers with salt and pepper. Place the tops and the peppers, cut side down, on the prepared baking sheet. Roast for 15 minutes, or until the peppers are soft and lightly browned. Flip the peppers, cut side up, and roast for another 5 minutes.

While the peppers are roasting, combine the rinsed quinoa and broth in a saucepan and bring to a boil over medium-high heat. Reduce the heat to low, cover, and simmer for 15 to 20 minutes, until the liquid is absorbed and the quinoa is fluffy. (If your quinoa is still slightly moist, you can spread it out on another baking sheet to dry.) Add the pesto and mix until combined.

Fill each bell pepper with ¼ cup of the pesto quinoa. Drizzle with olive oil, and season with salt and pepper. Place the top on each stuffed pepper and serve.

Zucchini Boats Filled with Pesto and Goat Cheese

MAKES 2 TO 4 SERVINGS

⏱ READY IN 45 MINUTES

2 medium to large zucchini

Salt and pepper, to taste

1 medium white or red onion, thinly sliced

1 bell pepper (any color), seeded and thinly sliced

1 tablespoon olive oil

½ cup crumbled goat cheese, at room temperature

½ cup pesto

¼ cup lightly toasted breadcrumbs (use panko for a crunchier texture)

Anyone who has ever grown zucchini knows they will eventually be left with the daunting task of figuring out what to do with all the extra zucchini at the end of the summer. Use this simple dish as inspiration, and serve it as either a main course at lunch or a side dish for dinner.

Preheat the oven to 400°F. Line a large rimmed baking sheet with parchment paper or lightly greased aluminum foil.

Cut each zucchini in half lengthwise. Using a small melon baller or spoon, scoop out the center seeds to create a shallow indentation. Season with salt and pepper.

Place the zucchini halves, cut side down, on half of the prepared baking sheet. Place the onion and bell pepper slices on the other half. Drizzle the olive oil over everything. Season the onion and bell pepper with salt and pepper. Using your hands or a large spoon, toss the onion and bell pepper together.

Roast for 15 minutes, flip over the zucchini, and roast for another 15 minutes. Remove the vegetables from the oven and let them cool for 5 minutes.

While the vegetables cool, blend the goat cheese and pesto in a small bowl.

Fill each zucchini boat with 2 to 4 tablespoons of the pesto mixture, depending on the size of the zucchini. Top with the onion and bell pepper. Finish with the breadcrumbs and serve.

Poultry

Jazzing up roasted chicken with a traditional pesto sauce is easy, quick, and tasty—but as you will learn in this chapter, there's also enormous opportunity to be inventive through personalized pesto. Here, explore options ranging from family meals to beautiful dinner parties.

Grilled Chicken Pesto Kebabs

½ cup pesto, such as Sun-Dried
   Tomato Pesto (page 30)
Juice of 2 limes
1 large boneless, skinless chicken
   breast, cut into 1½-inch pieces
1 zucchini, cut into 1-inch-thick
   half-moons
1 yellow squash, cut into 1-inch-
   thick half-moons
1 bell pepper (any color), seeded
   and cut into 1-inch squares
8 cherry tomatoes
1 tablespoon canola or peanut oil
Salt and pepper, to taste

Chicken is on regular rotation in our home. In order to keep things interesting, I like to serve kebabs because they offer flexibility. With a quick change of vegetables or marinade, I have a new and exciting dish each time. You can use 8- or 12-inch wooden skewers for these, depending on the portion size you'd like. For a complete meal, serve with pasta or rice—or try wrapping the skewered meat and veggies in a tortilla!

Preheat the oven to 450°F. Line a large rimmed baking sheet with lightly greased aluminum foil. Soak four to eight wooden skewers in water for 15 minutes.

Mix the pesto and lime juice together. Divide the pesto mixture between two large bowls. Put the chicken in one bowl, add a pinch of salt and pepper, and mix to coat. Put the zucchini, yellow squash, bell pepper, and tomatoes in the other bowl, season with salt and pepper, and mix to coat. Let the chicken and vegetables marinate in the pesto mixture for 10 minutes.

Transfer the marinated chicken to the prepared baking sheet. Bake for 5 minutes and remove them from the oven, but keep the oven on.

Assemble and thread the skewers, alternating vegetables and chicken.

Heat a cast iron grill pan over high heat and spray with cooking oil spray. You will know the grill pan is ready when you add a drop of water to it and it sizzles. Working in batches if necessary, place the skewers on the pan and cook for 2 minutes on all four sides, applying mild pressure. Transfer the grill pan to the oven and bake for 5 minutes, or until the vegetables are tender and the chicken is cooked through. Serve.

**CHICKEN PESTO
FRIED RICE** *page 154*

Chicken Pesto Fried Rice

MAKES 2 ENTRÉE SERVINGS OR 4 FIRST COURSE SERVINGS
⏱ READY IN 30 MINUTES
Pictured on previous page

1 boneless, skinless chicken breast,
   cut lengthwise into thin strips
1 garlic clove, minced
1 tablespoon grated fresh ginger
2 tablespoons peanut oil, divided
Salt and pepper, to taste
¼ cup pesto
2 scallions, thinly sliced, white and
   green parts separated
¼ cup grated carrot
¼ cup thinly sliced celery,
   including celery greens
2 cups cooked jasmine rice (see
   method on page 8), chilled
1 teaspoon toasted sesame seeds,
   for garnish
1 tablespoon crushed peanuts or
   cashews, for garnish

Who doesn't love fried rice? Once the prep is done, this dish comes together quickly. If you use a Thai-inspired pesto, you will feel like you are eating takeout without ever leaving home.

In a large bowl, combine the chicken, garlic, ginger, and 1 tablespoon of the oil. Season with salt and pepper and mix to combine.

Warm the remaining 1 tablespoon oil in a wok over medium-high heat. Add the chicken strips and stir-fry for 3 to 5 minutes, until golden. Transfer the chicken to a bowl. Add the pesto, scallion whites, carrot, celery, and a pinch of salt to the wok and stir-fry for 3 to 5 minutes.

Add the cooked rice and toss everything together. Return the cooked chicken to the wok and mix well.

Divide the chicken fried rice among two or four bowls. Garnish with the scallion greens, sesame seeds, and crushed nuts and serve.

Easy Baked Chicken Parmigiana

MAKES 2 SERVINGS

⏱ READY IN 45 MINUTES

2 boneless, skinless chicken breasts, pounded to ¼-inch thickness
Salt and pepper, to taste
½ cup Pesto Mayo (page 27)
1 teaspoon Dijon mustard
Juice of ½ lemon
½ cup breadcrumbs
¼ cup grated parmesan
4 slices mozzarella

I love to recreate classic dishes and lighten them up to make them more waistline friendly without losing any of the flavor. This version of chicken parmigiana is baked instead of fried, saving you not only calories but also time! Serve with bread and a salad to round out the meal.

Preheat the oven to 375°F. Line a small baking sheet with lightly greased aluminum foil.

Season the chicken with salt and pepper on both sides.

Mix the pesto mayo, mustard, and lemon juice in a bowl and transfer the mixture to a large, shallow dish or plate. Combine the breadcrumbs and parmesan on another plate.

Using a brush or one of your hands, coat each chicken breast with the pesto mixture. Transfer the breasts to the breadcrumb mixture and dredge to coat them on both sides.

Place the dredged chicken on the prepared baking sheet. Bake for 20 minutes. Flip over the chicken breasts, place 2 mozzarella slices on each one, and bake for an additional 10 minutes, until the cheese is melted and bubbling and the chicken is cooked through.

Remove the chicken from the oven. Let it rest for 10 minutes and then serve.

Sizzling Chicken Pesto Fajitas

MAKES 4 SERVINGS

⏱ READY IN 20 MINUTES

¼ cup Sun-Dried Tomato Pesto
  (page 30)
Grated zest and juice of 1 lime
2 garlic cloves, minced
¼ teaspoon ground cumin
¼ teaspoon cayenne pepper
¼ teaspoon red pepper flakes
Salt and pepper, to taste
1 boneless, skinless chicken breast,
  sliced into thin strips
2 tablespoons canola or peanut oil,
  divided
1 cup thinly sliced onion
2 cups thinly sliced bell pepper
  (any color)
4 (8-inch) tortillas
4 tablespoons Spicy Pesto Aioli
  (page 27), divided
Shredded Cotija or Manchego
  cheese, for garnish
Thinly sliced lettuce, for garnish
Cilantro leaves, for garnish
Avocado slices, for garnish

NOTE: If you are especially
crunched for time, pick up a rotisserie chicken at the market and
shred the chicken breast.

Dave and I used to frequent Willy's Mexicana Grill in Atlanta
to buy their delicious wraps, and this dish takes me right
back there in spirit! The addition of pesto makes these even
better. As an added bonus, this recipe is a great way to use up
leftovers.

Combine the pesto, lime zest and juice, garlic, cumin, cayenne
pepper, and red pepper flakes in a bowl. Season with salt and
pepper and mix to combine. Add the chicken and toss to coat.
Marinate for 10 minutes.

Warm 1 tablespoon of the oil in a grill pan over high heat. Add
the onion and cook, stirring occasionally, until soft, about 5
minutes. Push the onion to one side of the pan and add the
bell pepper. Cook, stirring occasionally, for another 5 minutes.
Transfer the onion and bell pepper to a bowl.

Add the remaining 1 tablespoon oil to the pan. Add the chicken
strips and marinade and cook for 7 minutes, or until the
chicken is cooked through. Return the onion and bell pepper
to the pan.

Meanwhile, warm the tortillas in the microwave for about 30
seconds.

To assemble the fajitas, lay out the tortillas on a clean work
surface. Spread 1 tablespoon of the pesto aioli on each tortilla. Top with some chicken, onion, and bell pepper. Garnish
with cheese, lettuce, cilantro leaves, and avocado. Fold the
fajitas, one side over the other, and eat as is or return to the
microwave for 10 to 15 seconds, until the cheese is melted and
everything is warmed throughout.

"One and Done" Chicken and Veggie Plate

MAKES 4 TO 6 SERVINGS

⏱ READY IN 30 MINUTES

1 large boneless, skinless chicken breast, cut into 1-inch pieces

1 large onion, cut into 1-inch pieces

1 yellow squash, cut into 1-inch pieces

1 zucchini, cut into 1-inch pieces

2 carrots, cut into 1-inch pieces

2 large potatoes, cut into 1-inch pieces

20 grape tomatoes, halved

½ cup Tangy Pesto Vinaigrette (page 26), plus more as desired

One bowl and one baking sheet—what could be easier or faster when life gets busy? All the ingredients come together very quickly to provide you with a fast, flavorful meal. This dish will pair well with leftover fried rice or rice pilaf.

Preheat the oven to 425°F. Line a large rimmed baking sheet with lightly greased aluminum foil.

Combine the chicken and vegetables in a large bowl. Pour in the pesto vinaigrette and mix to coat evenly.

Spread out the chicken and vegetables on the prepared baking sheet. Make sure there is space around each piece so everything cooks evenly. Roast for 25 to 30 minutes, until the vegetables caramelize and the chicken is cooked through.

Remove from the oven and serve.

Pesto Turkey Meatballs with Tomato Sauce

MAKES 4 TO 6 SERVINGS

⏱ **READY IN 2 HOURS (INCLUDES CHILLING TIME)**

2 garlic cloves, minced
½ cup finely chopped parsley
½ cup finely chopped spinach
2 tablespoons thinly sliced
    scallions
¾ cup ricotta cheese
½ cup breadcrumbs
¼ cup grated parmesan
¼ cup pesto
1 pound ground turkey
1½ teaspoons salt
1 tablespoon olive oil
4 cups Tomato Sauce (recipe
    follows)
1 pound spaghetti
Grated parmesan, for garnish

One of my favorite cookbooks is Julia Turshen's *Small Victories*. It never disappoints, with easy, delicious recipes. I have been making meatballs from way back and was delighted to try Julia's turkey meatballs, which include ricotta cheese. After trying her recipe, I've added this creamy addition to my own recipe.

In a large bowl, mix together the garlic, parsley, spinach, scallions, ricotta, breadcrumbs, parmesan, pesto, turkey, and salt. The mixture will be quite moist. Cover the bowl and place it in the refrigerator for 1 hour. (Chilling makes forming the balls much easier.)

Position a rack in the middle of the oven and preheat it to 425°F. Line a large rimmed baking sheet with lightly greased aluminum foil.

Form the mixture into round balls, using 2 tablespoons per ball. Transfer them to the prepared baking sheet and drizzle them with the oil. Bake for 20 to 25 minutes, until the turkey is cooked through.

While the meatballs are baking, warm the tomato sauce in a covered saucepan over medium-low heat.

When the meatballs are done, add them to the tomato sauce, cover the pan, reduce the heat to low, and simmer for 15 minutes.

Meanwhile, bring a large pot of water to a boil over medium-high heat. Add the spaghetti and cook until al dente. Reserve 1 cup of the pasta water to rehydrate the pasta if it looks dry. Drain and rinse.

When ready to serve, place a mound of pasta in the center of each plate and top with three to five meatballs and some tomato sauce. Garnish with grated parmesan and serve.

Tomato Sauce

MAKES APPROXIMATELY
3 CUPS

1 tablespoon olive oil
½ cup chopped onion
3 garlic cloves, minced
1 (28-ounce) can diced tomatoes
¼ cup torn basil leaves
Salt and pepper, to taste

Heat the oil in a 10-inch non-stick skillet over medium-high heat. Add the onion and garlic and cook, stirring frequently, until fragrant, 3 to 5 minutes. Add the tomatoes with their juices and the basil. Mash the tomatoes with a fork, lower the heat to low, and simmer for 15 minutes. Season with salt and pepper. Use immediately or store in an airtight container in the refrigerator for up to 4 days.

Seafood

From Hope's Gardens' former Atlanta headquarters to the
Atlantic coast was a four-hour drive—but the fresh-caught
scallops and shrimp always made it worth the trip. Here, we
recreate six of our most treasured fish- and crustacean-based
meals, developed over years of visiting the Georgia coastline.

Buttery Seared Sea Scallops over Green Tea Noodles

MAKES 4 SERVINGS
🕐 **READY IN 20 MINUTES**

7 ounces green tea noodles

4 tablespoons Compound Pesto Butter (page 29), 2 tablespoons reserved for garnish

½ cup breadcrumbs

1 tablespoon grated parmesan

¼ teaspoon grated lemon zest

1 pound sea scallops, side muscles removed

Salt and pepper, to taste

1 tablespoon olive oil, plus more to drizzle

For an exotic twist on an already elegant and luxurious dish, I use a pesto butter that highlights the sweet, delicate flavor of sea scallops (think lighter herb flavor, such as basil, dill, parsley, or even lemon or fennel). Look for scallops that are ivory or slightly pink in color. There are two varieties available: bay scallops, typically found in shallow waters, which are very small (about 100 per pound) and sea (or diver) scallops, which are found in deep, cold sea waters and are close to three times the size of bay scallops (20 to 30 per pound). Cooking times will vary when they are substituted in a recipe. Japanese green tea noodles complement this easy, fast dish nicely. If you are unable to find them, substitute spinach linguine or any noodle you like.

Bring a large pot of water to a boil over medium-high heat. Add the noodles and cook until al dente. Reserve 1 cup of the pasta water, then drain the noodles.

Warm the pesto butter in a small saucepan over medium heat.

Mix the breadcrumbs, parmesan, and lemon zest together. Toast the mixture in a small dry skillet over medium heat until golden. Remove from the heat.

Rinse the scallops and pat dry. Season both sides with salt and pepper. In a large nonstick skillet or a grill pan, warm the olive oil over medium-high heat. Add the scallops and sear on one side for 3 to 5 minutes. Flip the scallops and cook for another 3 minutes. Spoon the pesto butter over the scallops and then top with a sprinkle of the breadcrumb mixture.

To serve, divide the noodles evenly among four dishes. If the noodles look dry, add some of the reserved pasta water to rehydrate. Top with the scallops and garnish with the reserved pesto butter.

Pesto-Marinated Swordfish Kebabs

MAKES 4 SERVINGS

⏱ READY IN 30 MINUTES

2 tablespoons pesto

2 tablespoons olive oil

1 pound swordfish steaks, cut into 1¼-inch cubes

16 medium pearl onions

8 large button mushrooms

2 bell peppers (any color), seeded and cut into 4 (1-inch) pieces each

½ cup Classic Pesto Vinaigrette (page 26)

Salt and pepper, to taste

Swordfish is one of my family's favorite fish. I was looking for new ways to serve it to add variety to our meals. Kebabs are the perfect solution to your weeknight dinner blues. They are fun to serve and look elegant as well. Remember not to marinate your fish for any longer than 10 to 15 minutes, as the acids in the marinade may start to cook or break down the fish. Serve with a salad or rice alongside.

Preheat the oven to 400°F. Line two large rimmed baking sheets with parchment paper or lightly greased aluminum foil. Soak eight (8- or 12-inch) wooden skewers in water for 15 minutes.

Mix the pesto with the olive oil in a bowl. Add the swordfish cubes, toss to coat, and let marinate for 10 minutes.

While the swordfish is marinating, thread the vegetables onto four of the skewers in the following sequence: 2 pearl onions, 1 mushroom, 2 pieces of bell pepper, 1 mushroom, and 2 pearl onions. Transfer them to one of the prepared baking sheets.

Thread the marinated swordfish onto the remaining four skewers; place them on the other prepared baking sheet.

Pour the vinaigrette over the fish and the vegetables. Bake for 10 minutes, flip over the skewers, and bake for an additional 10 minutes.

Place one swordfish skewer and one vegetable skewer on each plate and serve.

Cedar-Wrapped Halibut
with Herbed Rice Pilaf

MAKES 4 SERVINGS
⏱ READY IN 30 MINUTES

2 Meyer lemons, each cut into 6 slices
½ medium sweet onion, thinly sliced
½ fennel bulb, thinly sliced
4 (4-ounce) halibut fillets
4 tablespoons pesto, divided
Salt and pepper, to taste
1 tablespoon canola or peanut oil
1 garlic clove
2 cups cooked jasmine rice (see method on page 8)
2 scallions, thinly sliced
½ cup mixed chopped herbs, such as dill, thyme, and/or oregano
Juice of 1 lemon
Toasted nuts, for garnish (any variety; see method on page 9)

Using cedar wraps is a great way to bring the taste of outdoor grilling inside. The wraps add a hint of smokiness to your fish. I purchase mine at Trader Joe's or Whole Foods. Often located close to the seafood department, they are plentiful during grilling season. If you are lucky enough to find Meyer lemons, which are a cross between a lemon and a mandarin orange, I suggest you try them instead of regular lemons, as they add a touch of sweetness to your dish.

Preheat the oven to 400°F. Line a large rimmed baking sheet with parchment paper. Soak four cedar wraps in water for at least 15 minutes. Cut four (12-inch) pieces of kitchen twine.

Remove the cedar wraps from the water, pat them dry, and lay them flat on a clean work surface. Place one piece of twine under each cedar wrap, centered. Overlap three slices of lemon in the middle of each wrap. Evenly divide the onion and fennel slices among the wraps. Place a piece of halibut on the veggies and spread 1 tablespoon of pesto on the halibut. Season with salt and pepper.

Fold one side of the cedar wrap over the other and use the twine to tie a bow to create a small bundle. Transfer the wraps to the prepared baking sheet. Bake for 10 minutes, remove from the oven, and let sit for another 5 minutes before un-wrapping.

While the fish is cooking, prepare the rice pilaf. Heat the oil in a nonstick skillet over medium heat. Using a zester, grate the garlic into the oil and let cook for 30 seconds. Add the rice, scallions, and herbs. Cover, lower the heat to low, and simmer for 10 minutes.

To serve, divide the rice pilaf among four plates. Remove the string from each cedar wrap and place the fish bundle next to the rice, or remove the cedar wrap entirely and place the fish and vegetables on top of the rice pilaf. Squeeze some lemon juice over each piece of fish and garnish with toasted nuts. Season with salt and pepper and serve.

Oven-Roasted Pesto-Glazed Salmon

MAKES 4 SERVINGS

⏱ READY IN 20 MINUTES

4 (6-ounce) salmon fillets
2 tablespoons lemon juice
¼ cup pesto
Grated zest of 1 lemon
¼ cup breadcrumbs
Salt and pepper, to taste

I have made this salmon dish so many times, I could do it with my eyes closed. It is so simple and always comes out great. Salmon pairs well with just about anything, but roasted vegetables or steamed asparagus are always a good choice.

Preheat the oven to 400°F. Line a large rimmed baking sheet with parchment paper.

Place the salmon fillets on the prepared baking sheet. Drizzle them with the lemon juice, then spread the pesto evenly on top of each fillet. Sprinkle with the lemon zest and breadcrumbs. Season with salt and pepper.

Bake for 10 minutes for medium-rare (pink, opaque, and juicy) or 12 minutes for medium (flaky and coral colored). Let sit for a few minutes and serve.

Southern-Style Pesto Shrimp over Cheesy Grits

MAKES 4 SERVINGS

⏱ READY IN 30 MINUTES

Pictured on following page

4 cups vegetable broth (see method on page 8), chicken broth, or water

1 cup stone-ground grits

1 tablespoon butter

1 cup shredded cheddar

Salt and pepper, to taste

¼ cup pesto

2 tablespoons lemon juice

2 tablespoons olive oil

1 pound large shrimp (31/35 count), peeled and deveined

3 slices bacon, cooked (see method on page 8) and crumbled

I spent over 20 years living down South, where one of the most popular restaurant dishes is shrimp and grits. My family is quite fond of it. In fact, every time I was out of town, Dave and Hope would prepare a big batch. Cooking the shrimp in pesto butter is always a winning idea. If you want more of that pesto goodness, swirl it into the grits as well.

Bring the broth to a boil in a large saucepan over medium-high heat. Add the grits and stir. When it returns to a boil, lower the heat to medium-low and cover. Cook, stirring every few minutes, for 10 to 15 minutes, until the mixture has thickened. Add the butter and cheese, stirring to combine. Season with salt and pepper.

Mix together the pesto, lemon juice, and olive oil. Combine the pesto mixture and the shrimp in a bowl, tossing until the shrimp are well coated.

Heat a large nonstick skillet over high heat. Add the pesto shrimp and cook, stirring occasionally, for 3 minutes, until the shrimp turn pink and are cooked through.

To serve, divide the grits evenly among four bowls. Divide the shrimp on top and garnish with the crumbled bacon.

**SOUTHERN-STYLE PESTO
SHRIMP OVER CHEESY
GRITS** *page 171*

Fish Tacos with Mango Salsa and Pesto Mayo

MAKES 8 TACOS

⊙ READY IN 20 MINUTES

1 tablespoon canola or peanut oil
4 (4-ounce) flaky, white fish fillets
Salt and pepper, to taste
8 (8-inch) flour tortillas
½ cup Pesto Mayo (page 27)
Mango Salsa (recipe follows)
2 cups shredded cheese (any
    variety), divided

Although I call for white fish fillets for this recipe, these tacos would be terrific with any leftover fish you might have from last night's dinner.

Heat the oil in a large nonstick skillet over medium-high heat. Season the fish with salt and pepper on both sides and add them to the skillet. Cook the fish for 3 minutes on one side. Flip them and cook for 3 minutes on the other side, or until the fish is cooked through. Transfer to a plate, either leaving the pieces intact or flaking them with a fork.

To assemble the tacos, lay the tortillas on a flat surface. On each, spread 1 tablespoon of the pesto mayo. Evenly distribute the fish and top with the salsa and cheese. If you'd like to melt the cheese, microwave for 10 seconds. Fold and serve.

Mango Salsa

MAKES 2 CUPS

1 ripe mango, peeled, pitted,
    and diced
1 teaspoon grated lime zest
2 tablespoons lime juice
2 tablespoons minced
    jalapeño
¼ cup minced red onion
1 garlic clove, minced

Combine all the ingredients in a bowl and mix well. Use immediately or store in an airtight container in the refrigerator for a day or so.

Beef, Pork, and Lamb

In our kitchen, meat is for special occasions—something to enjoy once or twice a month, at holidays, and with friends. When we entertain, we always work to integrate fresh ingredients from the garden, along with—you guessed it— pesto. These recipes are focused on meals to share.

Dave's Pesto-Glazed New York Strip Steak

MAKES 4 SERVINGS

⏱ READY IN 60 MINUTES

2 (1- to 1½-inch-thick) New York strip steaks

Salt and pepper, to taste

4 tablespoons Compound Pesto Butter (page 29), such as kale, at room temperature

2 large kale leaves, cut into thin strips

2 tablespoons minced shallots

1 tablespoon minced chives

1 garlic clove, minced

1 tablespoon canola or peanut oil

When we lived in Atlanta, I had very little to do with steak preparation–that was Dave's domain. With his grill and his music turned up high, he would disappear for a while, only to return with several perfectly grilled New York strip steaks. After they rested a bit, he skillfully sliced them on the diagonal. Since our move to New York City, I have discovered the beauty of cooking in a cast iron grill pan. Now, there are two steak masters in our home. Try serving these alongside the "Always Make Extra" Potatoes (page 139) or on top of a hearty salad. Always bring your meat to room temperature before cooking, as a cold piece of meat will cool down the pan or grill and won't produce a crisp sear.

Pat the steaks dry and season both sides with salt and pepper. Let them rest at room temperature for 30 minutes.

To make the herb pesto butter, combine the pesto butter, kale, shallots, chives, and garlic. Set aside.

Place a cast iron grill pan in a cold oven and preheat it to 500°F. Carefully remove the pan from the oven and place it over medium-high heat on the stovetop. Spray or brush the grill pan with the oil.

Place the steaks on the grill pan and cook for 2 minutes on one side. Flip the steaks and cook for 2 minutes on the other side. Lower the heat to medium and continue cooking and flipping every 2 minutes for 7 to 9 minutes, until an instant-read thermometer inserted into the thickest part of the meat registers 125°F for medium-rare. Transfer the steaks to a carving board. Coat the top of the meat with the herb pesto butter, which will melt into the steak. Tent the steaks with aluminum foil and let them rest for 10 minutes before slicing. Transfer the slices to a platter and serve.

Pesto-Stuffed Burgers

MAKES 4 BURGERS

⏱ **READY IN 20 MINUTES**

2 tablespoons butter

2 large onions, thinly sliced

1 pound ground beef

8 tablespoons pesto

Salt and pepper, to taste

4 sesame seed buns

1 cup shredded Gruyère, divided

1 avocado, pitted, peeled, and
   sliced

2 tablespoons Pesto Mayo
   (page 27)

Adding pesto to your ground beef will make this the tastiest and juiciest burger you have ever eaten. Once you taste this, you will never make your burgers without pesto again. Pull out a jar of crispy pickles and a bag of crunchy potato chips and you are in business!

In a nonstick skillet, melt the butter over medium heat. Add the onions and cook, stirring occasionally, until golden brown and caramelized, 10 to 12 minutes. Set aside.

Divide the meat into four even patties. Press each patty flat to a ¼-inch thickness. Top each with 2 tablespoons pesto. Season with salt and pepper. Fold the edges in toward the center to incorporate the pesto, then form the meat back into patties. Don't worry if the pesto seeps out a bit—it will still taste great.

Warm a cast iron grill pan over medium-high heat. Place the sesame seed buns, cut sides down, on the grill and toast lightly for 1 to 2 minutes. Remove from the pan. Spray the pan with cooking oil spray and add the patties. Cook for 3 minutes on each side for medium-rare (145°F).

To serve, arrange the bun bottoms on a platter. Place a patty on each bottom and top with caramelized onions, Gruyère, and avocado. Spread the pesto mayonnaise evenly on the bun tops. Place on top of the burgers and serve.

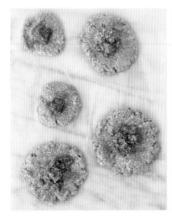 

Pesto Cream–Filled Flank Steak Roulade

MAKES 8 SERVINGS

⏱ READY IN 60 MINUTES

Pictured on page 184

½ cup pesto

½ cup sour cream

2 pounds flank steak

3 slices provolone

3 slices prosciutto

Salt and pepper, to taste

2 tablespoons olive oil, divided

1 red onion, thickly sliced

1 red bell pepper, seeded and
   thickly sliced

1 pound fingerling potatoes, halved

Flank steak is the perfect way to feed a crowd, and it tends to be inexpensive compared to other meats. This dish tastes so delicious and looks so impressive, no one will miss the beef tenderloin! Surround the roulade with vegetables to cook at the same time. Any will do; just make sure they are cut to a similar size so they cook thoroughly. I include directions for butterflying the steak, but you can also ask your butcher to do it for you.

Preheat the oven to 350°F. Lightly grease a 9 × 13-inch baking dish or oval gratin. Cut 6 (12-inch) pieces of kitchen twine.

Mix together the pesto and sour cream; set aside.

To butterfly the flank steak, insert the tip of a sharp knife at one long edge of the flank steak and slice horizontally, almost to the opposite edge, so that it opens up like a book. Make sure not to cut the steak into two separate pieces. Place a piece of wax paper over the open steak and use a meat mallet to pound the steak to an even thickness, about ¼ inch thick. This will also help tenderize the meat. Discard the wax paper.

Spread the pesto cream over the butterflied flank steak. Top with overlapping slices of provolone, followed by overlapping slices of prosciutto. Season with salt and pepper. With the long edge of the steak facing you, roll it up and secure it with a piece of kitchen twine every 1½ inches. Drizzle 1 tablespoon of the olive oil over the top and season with salt and pepper.

Place the steak in the prepared baking dish. Scatter the vegetables around the meat. Drizzle the vegetables with the remaining 1 tablespoon olive oil. Roast for 40 to 45 minutes, until an instant-read thermometer inserted into the thickest part of the meat registers 125°F to 130°F for medium-rare.

Transfer the steak to a cutting board and let it rest for 10 minutes. Remove the twine, slice the steak into medallions, and serve.

READY TO ROLL: The butterflied flank steak with its goodies

GIVE IT A REST: When the steak is cooked (above), transfer it to a cutting board to rest before cutting.

PESTO CREAM–FILLED FLANK STEAK ROULADE *page 182*

BACON-WRAPPED PESTO-GLAZED PORK TENDERLOIN WITH ROASTED VEGETABLES *page 186*

Bacon-Wrapped Pesto-Glazed Pork Tenderloin with Roasted Vegetables

MAKES 4 SERVINGS

⏱ READY IN 45 MINUTES

Pictured on previous page

8 slices bacon

1 pound pork tenderloin

½ cup pesto

Salt and pepper, to taste

Maple syrup, to drizzle

Olive oil, to drizzle

2 large potatoes, cut into 1½-inch
   pieces

2 large carrots, cut into 1½-inch
   pieces

I can think of nothing better with pork than adding more pork! If you have never tried maple syrup on your bacon, you will be pleasantly surprised at how well the flavors marry. Cooking the vegetables alongside the pork makes this recipe a one-pan wonder.

Preheat the oven to 350°F. Line a 9 × 13-inch baking dish or oval gratin with aluminum foil. Cut 6 (12-inch) pieces of kitchen twine.

On a flat surface, arrange the bacon slices so that they overlap on their long edges. Place the tenderloin horizontally on top in the center of the bacon. Cover the entire tenderloin with the pesto. Season with salt and pepper. Wrap the bacon slices around the pork. Slide the twine underneath the meat and secure it by tying the twine every 1½ inches. Drizzle with maple syrup and olive oil. Season with salt and pepper.

Warm a nonstick skillet over medium heat. Transfer the wrapped pork to the skillet and sear for 3 minutes on the top and bottom sides. Transfer the pork to the prepared baking dish. Surround the tenderloin with the vegetables. Roast for 20 minutes, or until an instant-read thermometer inserted into the thickest part of the pork registers 140°F to 145°F. Watch carefully, as the tenderloin cooks quickly and can easily go from perfect to overcooked in a few minutes.

Transfer the pork to a cutting board. Let it rest for 10 minutes, then remove the twine. Slice the pork into medallions and transfer them to a serving platter. Surround the pork with the roasted vegetables and serve.

THE ASSEMBLED TENDERLOIN: Use kitchen twine to secure the bacon.

AFTER SEARING: The pork and veggies are ready for the oven.

TEMPERATURE CHECK: Make sure the thermometer reads between 140°F and 145°F.

Pesto Sausage Lettuce Wraps

MAKES 8 WRAPS

⏱ **READY IN 20 MINUTES**

2 tablespoons olive oil

1 medium red onion, chopped

½ fennel bulb, chopped

1 bell pepper (any color), seeded and chopped

4 sweet Italian sausages (about 1 pound total), casings removed

½ cup pesto

8 large lettuce leaves, such as Boston or Bibb

2 cups cooked rice (see method on page 8) or other grain

Sausage with peppers and onions is a classic Italian dish. I make this even more Italian by adding pesto. Swapping the buns for lettuce leaves makes a healthier version of an old favorite.

Heat the olive oil in a nonstick skillet over medium-high heat. Add the red onion, fennel, and pepper. Cook, stirring occasionally, until they soften, 5 to 7 minutes. Add the sausage, breaking it up in the pan with the back of a wooden spoon or a potato masher, and cook for 5 minutes. Add the pesto and cook for another 5 to 7 minutes, until the sausage is cooked through.

To assemble the wraps, lay out the lettuce leaves on a flat surface. Divide the cooked rice evenly among them, followed by the pesto sausage mixture. Roll up each leaf like a burrito and serve. Have plenty of napkins ready, as they can be messy to eat!

**MINT PESTO
LAMB
KEBABS WITH
COUSCOUS**
page 192

Mint Pesto Lamb Kebabs with Couscous

MAKES 4 OR 8 KEBABS

⏱ READY IN 40 MINUTES

Pictured on previous page

8 ounces Israeli couscous (pearl couscous)

3 tablespoon olive oil

1½ cups hot water

½ cup golden raisins

½ cup pistachios

¼ cup mint leaves, cut into thin strips

4 tablespoons Mint Pesto (see page 31), divided

2 tablespoons white wine vinegar

2 tablespoons lemon juice

1 pound boneless lamb loin, cut into 1¼-inch cubes

2 tablespoons plain Greek yogurt

Salt and pepper, to taste

Atlanta is a town known for its great love of food. After 20-plus years living there, we found a few great dining spots that were perfect for large gatherings and celebrations. One of our favorites was Rumi's Kitchen, a Persian restaurant with the most beautiful and flavorful kebab offerings. I created this recipe because it reminds me of one of our most cherished memories there—our daughter Hope's high school graduation. I hope this becomes one of your favorite dishes to share with family and friends.

Preheat the oven to 425°F. Line a large rimmed baking sheet with lightly greased aluminum foil. Soak 4 to 8 (8- or 12-inch) wooden skewers in water for 15 minutes.

Combine the couscous and 1 tablespoon of the olive oil in a saucepan; cook over medium heat, stirring occasionally, for 5 minutes, or until the couscous turns a golden color. Add the hot water and bring to a boil. Turn the heat to low, cover, and simmer for 12 minutes, or until the liquid is absorbed. Remove from the heat. Add the raisins, pistachios, and mint, stirring to combine.

Meanwhile, in a large bowl, mix together 2 tablespoons of the mint pesto, the vinegar, lemon juice, and remaining 2 tablespoons olive oil. Add the lamb cubes and let them marinate at room temperature for 10 to 15 minutes.

Thread three to five lamb cubes on each soaked skewer. Transfer them to the prepared baking sheet. Roast for 10 minutes, or until an instant-read thermometer inserted into the thickest part of the lamb registers 145°F for medium-rare.

While the lamb is cooking, mix the yogurt with the remaining 2 tablespoons mint pesto and stir well.

To serve, scoop a large spoonful of the couscous onto the center of each plate. Top with one or two lamb skewers. Drizzle the mint pesto yogurt over the top. Season with salt and pepper.

Finished couscous awaiting the the cooked kebabs.

Oven-ready threaded lamb kebabs.

Acknowledgments

A FEW YEARS AGO, my family returned to New York, my birthplace. I was in the throes of a new chapter in life—the empty nest. It was a perfect time to focus on learning everything I could about writing a cookbook and meeting as many people as I could that were involved in similar pursuits, as well as those with a great love of food. I have loved being a student again and working diligently on my "thesis." During the course of writing and developing the recipes in this cookbook, my family and I have eaten more than our fair share of delicious food. We have explored the farmers markets, discovered the different neighborhoods of New York, and met and worked with an exceptional group of people.

This process has been a true labor of love. Very few labor without support from others. I have been fortunate to have so many people who have contributed to this book and to any successes I have scored.

I wish to thank:

My family. Dave, you have always been by my side, encouraging me to go for-

Hope and Dave.

ward with all the crazy ideas I dream up. Together we have journeyed down many roads, having fun and learning some pretty cool things in the process. This will continue! You and your garden goodies inspired so many of the recipes throughout this book. Lastly, a big thank-you for writing the section on growing basil. You were always so happy in your garden, and in addition, you have put your writing skills and college English degree to work.

Hope, you have inspired and amazed me from day one. Today, seeing the woman you have become, I am so proud. You have been a great design guru to me, and I only expect

that to grow. I have a lot to learn from you. Being in New York with you is more than I could ask for. I love that you love this city as much as, if not more than, I do.

Mommy (yes, I still call my mother Mommy), you always had dinner on the table for us, even when Nancy and I were working in the city and getting home after 9 p.m. I have learned so much from watching you in the kitchen since I was a child. One of those things, preparing dinner at 6 a.m. before anyone was up in the house, has become my way as well. I am so happy to be close by you again after 20 years down South.

Leslie and her mother, Roberta.

The Recipe Tester Group: Tia Adler and Laura Wyckoff (two of my closest friends since childhood), Caryn Kramer, Maryann O'Keefe, Galita Leiderman, Karla Salinari, Steve Hurlburt, Laura Allen, Virginia Summerell, Betsy Alterman, my wonderful brother-in-law Doug Lennox, Max Roll, Karen and Benno Rothschild, and Laurie Kratz. Without your help and great feedback, I would not have known if anyone other than myself would be able to follow my directions and produce a wonderful dish featuring a personalized pesto. Thank you, and I hope you will continue to use these recipes time and time again, putting your own spin on them.

To my sister, Nancy, and my womyn (our little joke) Betsy, thank you for being my guinea pigs in our early years living on East 46th Street, where I perfected pasta primavera night after night! That was the start of my love to cook for others.

To Cillar Serrant, Carmen Alcee, Diedre (Deedee) Godbold, and Magnita (Maggie) Hughes, you ladies are like family to my mother, sister, and me. Without your love and care for our mother, I do not think I would have been able to put in all the time necessary to create this cookbook.

Jenni Ferrari-Adler, my agent, thank you for taking a chance on an unknown quantity who you met for 3 minutes at the Food Book Fair's "Literary Speed Dating" event. Your perseverance is much appreciated.

To Jessica Marx, working with you on the test photographs for my book proposal was such a wonderful experience. You are so talented and also a lot of fun to spend an afternoon working and eating with. Together, we were able to capture the beauty and deliciousness of several of my pesto recipes, which contributed to finding an agent and a publisher. Thank you.

To Rose O'Donoghue, you are a dream come true. You answered my posting and I knew as soon as I read your resume that we would work well together. Thank you for your work ethic, for your skills in the kitchen and on paper, and for becoming a wonderful new friend.

To Lila Allen Davis, I first met you when you were 4 or 5; you were a beautiful flower girl in our wedding. Watching you grow up and become the incredibly talented writer and editor you are today is a great pleasure. You have been instrumental in making this book a reality—from helping me craft the proposal to editing the final manuscript. I could not have done this without you. Thank you.

To Jessica Easto, managing editor, and Morgan Krehbiel, design and production manager at Agate Publishing, you ladies have been exceptional to work with. You both have taught me so much, walked me through the process, and have been honest to a fault. I have enjoyed every moment working on this cookbook with you both. Thank you! And to everyone else at Agate / Surrey Books that I may not have met but have contributed to the completion of this cookbook a big thank you. I am so very proud of how it turned out. And lastly, thank you to Anna Repp for the exquisite illustrations throughout the book. 🍃

Kitchen Resources

US EQUIVALENCIES

tea-spoon	table-spoon	fluid ounce	cup	pint	quart	gallon
3	1	½	1/16	1/32	-	-
6	2	1	⅛	1/16	1/32	-
12	4	2	¼	⅛	1/16	-
18	6	3	⅜	-	-	-
24	8	4	½	¼	⅛	1/32
36	12	6	¾	-	-	-
48	16	8	1	½	¼	1/16
96	32	16	2	1	½	⅛
-	64	32	4	2	1	¼
-	256	128	16	8	4	1

OVEN TEMPERATURES

Oven Level	Fahrenheit	Celsius	British Gas Mark
Warming foods	200° to 250°	93° to 121°	0 to ¼
Very low	250° to 275°	121° to 133°	½ to 1
Low	300° to 325°	149° to 163°	2 to 3
Moderate	350° to 375°	177° to 190°	4 to 5
Hot	400° to 425°	204° to 218°	6 to 7
Very hot	450° to 475°	232° to 246°	8 to 9
Extremely hot	500° to 525°	260° to 274°	10

RECOMMENDED SAFE COOKING TEMPERATURES

Cooking to recommended temperatures kills harmful microorganisms. These temperatures fall within USDA-approved guidelines unless otherwise noted. Note that these temperatures are before resting. Meat continues to cook while resting off heat. The USDA recommends that steaks, chops, and roasts–from beef, pork, veal, or lamb–and fresh or smoked uncooked ham rest for at least 3 minutes before serving. Note that professional kitchens tend to cook to lower temperatures.

METRIC EQUIVALENTS (VOLUME)

US	Metric
¼ teaspoon	1 milliliter
½ teaspoon	2.5 milliliter
¾ teaspoon	4 milliliter
1 teaspoon	5 milliliter
1½ teaspoons	7.5 milliliter
2 teaspoons	10 milliliter
1 tablespoon	15 milliliter
2 tablespoons	30 milliliter
¼ cup	59 milliliter
⅓ cup	79 milliliter
½ cup	118 milliliter
⅔ cup	158 milliliter
¾ cup	178 milliliter
1 cup	237 milliliter
1½ cups	355 milliliter
2 cups (1 pint)	473 milliliter
3 cups	710 milliliter
4 cups (1 quart)	.95 liter
1.06 quarts	1 liter
4 quarts (1 gallon)	3.8 liters

METRIC EQUIVALENTS (WEIGHT)

US	Metric
.035 ounce	1 gram
.25 ounce	7 grams
.50 ounce	14 grams
.75 ounce	21 grams
1 ounce	28 grams
1.5 ounces	42.5 grams
2 ounces	57 grams
3 ounces	85 grams
4 ounces	113 grams
5 ounces	142 grams
6 ounces	170 grams
7 ounces	198 grams
8 ounces	227 grams
16 ounces (1 pound)	454 grams
2.2 pounds	1 kilogram

GLOSSARY OF COOKING TERMS

My recipes are not heavy on technique, and they often rely on spontaneity. One of my favorite sayings is "less is more"– less technique, more time. Still, it is important to know basic cooking and knife techniques, and I use the terms below often in this book.

Bake. To cook food in an oven, which surrounds it with dry heat. Generally speaking, baking occurs at relatively low temperatures (325°F to 375°F). Items are sometimes baked covered, which distinguishes it from roasting, in which items are never covered.

Blanch. To plunge foods quickly into boiling water, then into cold water. Fruits and vegetables are most often blanched. It can brighten color, add crispness and texture, or help you remove skins.

Boil. To cook food in water or other liquid that has been heated until bubbles break the surface.

Broil. To cook food in an oven near a direct heat source. Your oven's broiler may be at the top or bottom of the appliance, depending on the model.

Caramelize. To cook food slowly until its sugars have browned, creating a sweet flavor.

Chop. To cut food into bite-size or smaller pieces. The pieces should all be about the same size, but it's okay if they are uneven. Chopped food is bigger than minced food.

Cut crosswise. To cut food in the short direction, or around its circumference.

Cut lengthwise. To cut food in the long direction, or from pole to pole.

Dash. A small amount of a liquid, generally considered to be between 1/16 and 1/8 teaspoon. (See also: pinch)

Dice. To cut food into small (1/4-inch), medium (1/2-inch), or large (3/4-inch or larger) cubes.

Drain. To remove liquid from solid food, such as with a colander. When you drain, you discard the liquid and keep the solids. (See also: strain)

Emulsion. A combination of two liquids that do not normally mix, such as oil and water. By adding them together slowly while whisking or blending quickly, they bond.

Florets. The small flower-shaped parts of broccoli or cauliflower.

Garnish. An edible decoration to finish a dish.

Grease. To rub or spray oil or butter on a pan to prevent prepared food from sticking.

Julienne. To cut food, often vegetables, into thin matchstick strips.

Knead. To mix dough by pressing, folding, and pushing away from you with your hands in order to form it into a workable mass.

Mince. To cut food into very small pieces. Minced food is smaller than chopped food.

Ovenproof. Refers to a cooking utensil or pan that can be used in the oven.

Oxidize. To combine with oxygen. In the case of food, this tends to mean some kind of physical reaction has occurred, such as the darkening that can happen to pesto if it's exposed to the air.

Pinch. A small amount of a dry seasoning, generally considered to be between 1/16 and 1/8 teaspoon. (See also: dash)

Reserve. To set aside for later use.

Roast. To cook food (often proteins and vegetables) in an oven, which surrounds it with dry heat, in a shallow, uncovered pan, usually at relatively high temperatures (400°F and higher). Roasting produces a characteristic well-browned exterior and a tender interior.

Sauté. To cook food quickly in a small amount of fat in a skillet or sauté pan over direct heat, such as on the stove.

Savory. Spicy, salty taste and aroma. Also referred to as umami.

Simmer. To cook food gently in water or other liquid that has been heated until bubbles just begin to break the surface. Temperatures must be relatively low for this.

Strain. To remove liquid from solid food, such as with a sieve. When you strain, you discard the solids and keep the liquid. (See also: drain)

Well. A shallow indentation created to insert another ingredient.

Zest. The outer layer of citrus peel, not including the bitter white pith beneath.

PESTO WORKSHEETS

As you experiment with different flavor medleys for your homemade pesto, you're likely to run across some new favorites that you'll want to make again. Recreating favorites is a breeze with these worksheets, where you can record combinations of herbs, cheeses, nuts, vegetables, and other ingredients.

A Sharpie-style pen works best on this paper. Photocopy these pages for additional worksheets.

Suggested ratios

4 cups **plants**

½ cup **cheese***

½ cup **oil**

⅓ cup **nuts/seeds***

2+ **garlic cloves***

¼ teaspoon each **seasoning/acid**

optional

RECIPE NAME

_____

INGREDIENTS USED

Plants

Cheese

Oil

Nuts/seeds

Garlic

Seasoning/acid

NOTES

_____

_____

_____

RECIPE NAME

_____

INGREDIENTS USED

Plants

Cheese

Oil

Nuts/seeds

Garlic

Seasoning/acid

NOTES

_____

_____

_____

RECIPE NAME

_____

INGREDIENTS USED

Plants

Cheese

Oil

Nuts/seeds

Garlic

Seasoning/acid

NOTES

_____

_____

_____

RECIPE NAME

_____

INGREDIENTS USED

Plants _____

Cheese _____

Oil _____

Nuts/seeds _____

Garlic _____

Seasoning/acid _____

NOTES

_____

_____

_____

RECIPE NAME

_____

INGREDIENTS USED

Plants _____

Cheese _____

Oil _____

Nuts/seeds _____

Garlic _____

Seasoning/acid _____

NOTES

_____

_____

_____

RECIPE NAME

_____

INGREDIENTS USED

Plants _____

Cheese _____

Oil _____

Nuts/seeds _____

Garlic _____

Seasoning/acid _____

NOTES

_____

_____

_____

RECIPE NAME

_____

INGREDIENTS USED

Plants _____

Cheese _____

Oil _____

Nuts/seeds _____

Garlic _____

Seasoning/acid _____

NOTES

_____

_____

_____

RECIPE NAME

_____

INGREDIENTS USED

Plants _____

Cheese _____

Oil _____

Nuts/seeds _____

Garlic _____

Seasoning/acid _____

NOTES _____

_____

_____

RECIPE NAME

_____

INGREDIENTS USED

Plants _____

Cheese _____

Oil _____

Nuts/seeds _____

Garlic _____

Seasoning/acid _____

NOTES _____

_____

_____

RECIPE NAME

_____

INGREDIENTS USED

Plants _____

Cheese _____

Oil _____

Nuts/seeds _____

Garlic _____

Seasoning/acid _____

NOTES _____

_____

_____

RECIPE NAME

_____

INGREDIENTS USED

Plants _____

Cheese _____

Oil _____

Nuts/seeds _____

Garlic _____

Seasoning/acid _____

NOTES _____

_____

_____

Recipe Index

Chapter 1: The Modern Mother Sauce (Pesto Basics)

Classic Basil Pesto | 23

Thai-Inspired Pesto Vinaigrette | 26

Classic Pesto Vinaigrette | 26

Tangy Pesto Vinaigrette | 26

Pesto Mayo | 27

Spicy Pesto Aioli | 27

Buttermilk Pesto Dressing | 27

Kale Pesto Dressing | 27

Compound Pesto Butter | 29

Roasted Jalapeño-Cilantro Pesto | 30

Sun-Dried Tomato Pesto | 30

Mint Pesto | 31

Kale Pesto | 31

Olive Pesto | 32

Green Goddess Pesto | 32

Chapter 2: Eggs and Toasts

Green Eggs and Ham in a Shell | 41

Crowd-Pleasing Mini Quiches | 43

Pesto Omelette Your Way | 44

Avocado Pesto Toast | 45

Pesto Shakshuka | 48

 Green Shakshuka

 Red Shakshuka

Pesto Polenta with Poached Eggs in Pepper Rounds | 50

Chapter 3: Pastas and Pizzas

Spicy Thai-Inspired Noodles | 56

Pesto Lasagna | 56

Baked Pesto Risotto | 58

Butternut Squash Ravioli with Pesto Sauce | 59

Pesto Pasta Trilogy | 62

 Roasted Broccoli Orecchiette

 Roasted Beet and Blood Orange Pappardelle

 Fennel Capellini

Ode to ABC Pizza | 65

Naan Pizza with Fig and Jalapeño Pesto | 66

Sweet Roasted Date Flatbread | 68

Bountiful Cauliflower Crust Pizza | 73

Caprese Calzone | 74

Chapter 4: Sandwiches, Paninis, Bruschetta, and Crostini

Pesto Tea Sandwiches | 79

  Rainbow Pesto Tea Sandwiches

  Egg Salad and Pesto Tea Sandwiches

  Open-Faced Cucumber Pesto Sandwiches

  Open-Faced Red Radish and Pesto Sandwiches

  Open-Faced Smoked Salmon Pesto Sandwiches

The Gouda Goodness BLAT | 82

Mediterranean Roasted Veggie Sandwich | 84

Green Goddess Pesto Grilled Cheese | 87

Philadelphia Cheese Steak Pesto Wraps | 88

The Day after Thanksgiving Sandwich | 89

Pesto Crostini and Bruschetta Party | 91

  Kale Pesto and Shiitake Mushroom Crostini

  Roasted Lemon and Pesto Crostini

  Roasted Carrot Bruschetta

  Spicy Pesto Shrimp Bruschetta

Chapter 5: Appetizers and Small Bites

Silky Pesto Goat Cheese Terrine | 96

Cool Cucumber Bites with Shrimp Salad | 98

Grilled Eggplant Roll-Ups with Spicy Pesto Aioli | 100

Pesto-Stuffed Mushroom Caps | 101

Spicy Jalapeño Guacamole | 102

The Devil May Care Eggs | 105

Creamy Pesto Hummus with Cut Vegetables | 106

Pesto-Drizzled Grilled Chicken Satay | 109

Skewered Hors d'Oeuvres Platter | 110

  Caprese Skewers

  Shrimp Skewers

  Tortellini Skewers

Chapter 6: Soups

Gazpacho Shooters with Chilled Pesto Cubes | 114

Pesto Minestrone for All Seasons | 116

Chicken Pesto Noodle Soup | 117

Pesto Ramen Bowl | 118

Tri-Color Roasted Veggie Soup Bar | 122

  Roasted Carrot and Butternut Squash Soup

  Roasted Broccoli Potato Soup

  Roasted Beet and Bean Soup

Pesto Pork Wonton Soup | 125

Chapter 7: Vegetables

Heartbeet Salad with Orange-Honey Mustard Vinaigrette | 129

Seasonal Salads with Pesto Dressings and Homemade Croutons | 132

  Summer Greens with Buttermilk Pesto Dressing

  Winter Greens with Kale Pesto Dressing

Caprese Salad with Pesto Vinaigrette | 134

Ultimate Veggie Collard Wraps | 137

Prosciutto-Wrapped Asparagus Spears | 138

Chapter 8: Poultry

Grilled Chicken Pesto Kebabs | 151

Chicken Pesto Fried Rice | 154

Easy Baked Chicken Parmigiana | 155

Sizzling Chicken Pesto Fajitas | 157

"One and Done" Chicken and Veggie Plate | 158

Pesto Turkey Meatballs with Tomato Sauce | 160

Chapter 9: Seafood

Buttery Seared Sea Scallops over Green Tea Noodles | 165

Pesto-Marinated Swordfish Kebabs | 167

Cedar-Wrapped Halibut with Herbed Rice Pilaf | 168

Oven-Roasted Pesto-Glazed Salmon | 170

Southern-Style Pesto Shrimp over Cheesy Grits | 171

Fish Tacos with Mango Salsa and Pesto Mayo | 175

Chapter 10: Beef, Pork, and Lamb

Dave's Pesto-Glazed New York Strip Steak | 178

Pesto-Stuffed Burgers | 180

Pesto Cream-Filled Flank Steak Roulade | 182

Bacon-Wrapped Pesto-Glazed Pork Tenderloin with Roasted Vegetables | 186

Pesto Sausage Lettuce Wraps | 189

Mint Pesto Lamb Kebabs with Couscous | 192

"Always Make Extra" Potatoes with Savory Pesto Butter | 139

Cubed Butternut Squash over Pesto Zucchini Noodles | 140

Butternut Squash Spaghetti | 143

Leaning Eggplant Towers | 144

Pesto Quinoa-Stuffed Roasted Red Peppers | 146

Zucchini Boats Filled with Pesto and Goat Cheese | 147

Index

A

ABC Pizza, Ode to, 65
Acid, as basic pesto ingredient, 19
Almonds
    Kale Pesto, 31
    Mint Pesto, 31
"Always Make Extra" Potatoes
    with Savory Pesto Butter, 139
Anchovies
    Green Goddess Pesto, 32
    Olive Pesto, 32
Arugula
    about: pesto variation, 24
    Pesto Minestrone for All
        Seasons, 116
    Sweet Roasted Date
        Flatbread, 68
Asiago, in Spicy Pesto Shrimp
    Bruschetta, 93
Asparagus, Prosciutto-Wrapped
    Spears, 138
Avocado
    Gouda Goodness BLAT, 82
    Pesto Toast, 45
    Pesto-Stuffed Burgers, 180
    Spicy Jalapeño Guacamole, 102

B

Bacon
    about: cooking of, 8
    Bacon-Wrapped Pesto-
        Glazed Pork Tenderloin with
        Roasted Vegetables, 186
    Day after Thanksgiving
        Sandwich, 89
    Gouda Goodness BLAT, 82
    Green Eggs and Ham in a
        Shell, 41
    Pesto Omelette Your Way, 44
    Southern-Style Pesto Shrimp
        over Cheesy Grits, 171
Baguettes
    Kale Pesto and Shiitake
        Mushroom Crostini, 91
    Roasted Lemon and Pesto
        Crostini, 92

Baked Pesto Risotto, 58
Basil
    about: health benefits of, 13
    Caprese Salad with Pesto
        Vinaigrette, 134
    Caprese Skewers, 110
    Classic Basil Pesto, 23
    Green Goddess Pesto, 32
    Red Shakshuka, 49
    Tomato Sauce, 160
Basil, growing at home, 33
    from cuttings, 34, 36
    harvesting of leaves, 37
    from seeds planted outside,
        36-37
    from seeds started indoors, 34
    from starter plant outside, 37
Basil pesto
    about: basic ingredients of,
        13; history of, 12-13
    Classic, 23
Beans
    Creamy Pesto Hummus with
        Cut Vegetables, 106
    Pesto Minestrone for All
        Seasons, 116
    Roasted Beet and Bean Soup,
        124
Béchamel, about, 12
Beef
    Dave's Pesto-Glazed New
        York Strip Steak, 178
    Pesto Cream-Filled Flank
        Steak Roulade, 182
    Pesto-Stuffed Burgers, 180
    Philadelphia Cheese Steak
        Pesto Wraps, 88
Beets
    Heartbeet Salad with Orange
        Honey Mustard Vinaigrette,
        129
    Roasted Beet and Bean Soup,
        124
    Roasted Beet and Blood
        Orange Pappardelle, 63
    Ultimate Veggie Collard
        Wraps, 137

Bell peppers
    Bountiful Cauliflower Crust
        Pizza, 73
    Crowd-Pleasing Mini Quiches,
        43
    Gazpacho Shooters with
        Pesto Cubes, 114
    Grilled Chicken Pesto Kebabs,
        151
    Mediterranean Roasted
        Veggie Sandwich, 84
    Pesto Cream-Filled Flank
        Steak Roulade, 182
    Pesto Omelette Your Way, 44
    Pesto Polenta with Poached
        Eggs in Pepper Rounds, 50
    Pesto Quinoa-Stuffed
        Roasted Red Peppers, 146
    Pesto Ramen Bowl, 118
    Pesto Sausage Lettuce Wraps,
        189
    Pesto-Marinated Swordfish
        Kebabs, 167
    Philadelphia Cheese Steak
        Pesto Wraps, 88
    Red Shakshuka, 49
    Sizzling Chicken Pesto Fajitas,
        157
    Ultimate Veggie Collard
        Wraps, 137
    Zucchini Boats Filled with
        Pesto and Goat Cheese, 147
BLAT, Gouda Goodness, 82
Blood Orange, Roasted Beet and,
    Pappardelle, 63
Bountiful Cauliflower Crust Pizza,
    73
Bread
    Day after Thanksgiving
        Sandwich, 89
    Egg Salad and Pesto Tea
        Sandwiches, 81
    Gazpacho Shooters with
        Pesto Cubes, 114
    Gouda Goodness BLAT, 82
    Green Goddess Pesto Grilled
        Cheese, 87

INDEX   **205**

Homemade Croutons, 133
Open-Faced Red Radish and
    Pesto Sandwiches, 81
Rainbow Pesto Tea
    Sandwiches, 80
Roasted Carrot Bruschetta,
    93
Spicy Pesto Shrimp
    Bruschetta, 93
see also Baguettes;
    Bruschetta; Flatbread
Bread, pumpernickel cocktail
Open-Faced Cucumber Pesto
    Sandwiches, 81
Open-Faced Smoked Salmon
    Pesto Sandwiches, 81
Bread, rustic
about, 5
Avocado Pesto Toast, 45
Green Goddess Pesto Grilled
    Cheese, 87
Broccoli
Roasted Broccoli Orecchiette,
    62
Roasted Broccoli Potato
    Soup, 123
Broths, 6
making of, 8
using a variety of, 58
see also Vegetable broth
Bruschetta
Roasted Carrot, 93
Spicy Pesto Shrimp, 93
Brussels sprouts
Ode to ABC Pizza, 65
Pesto Ramen Bowl, 118
Burgers, Pesto-Stuffed, 180
Butter, using unsalted, 6
Buttermilk Pesto Dressing
recipe for, 27
Summer Greens with, 132
Butternut squash
Cubed, over Pesto Zucchini
    Noodles, 140
Mediterranean Roasted
    Veggie Sandwich, 84
Ravioli with Pesto Sauce, 59
Roasted Carrot and, Soup, 123
Spaghetti, 143
Buttery Seared Sea Scallops over
    Green Tea Noodles, 165

C

Cabbage, in Pesto Pork Wonton
    Soup, 125
Cajun flavor profiles, 21
Calzone, Caprese, 74
Candied nuts, in Cubed Butternut
    Squash over Pesto Zucchini
    Noodles, 140
Cannellini beans, in Creamy Pesto
    Hummus with Cut Vegetables,
    106
Capellini
    Chicken Pesto Noodle Soup,
        117
    Fennel Capellini, 63
    Leaning Eggplant Towers, 144
Capers
    Olive Pesto, 32
    Sun-Dried Tomato Pesto, 30
Caprese Calzone, 74
Caprese Salad with Pesto
    Vinaigrette, 134
Caprese Skewers, 110
Carrots
    Bacon-Wrapped Pesto-
        Glazed Pork Tenderloin with
        Roasted Vegetables, 186
    Chicken Pesto Fried Rice, 154
    Chicken Pesto Noodle Soup,
        117
    "One and Done" Chicken and
        Veggie Plate, 158
    Pesto Minestrone for All
        Seasons, 116
    Pesto Ramen Bowl, 118
    Roasted Carrot and Butternut
        Squash Soup, 123
    Roasted Carrot Bruschetta, 93
    Spicy Thai-Inspired Noodles,
        55
    Ultimate Veggie Collard
        Wraps, 137
Cauliflower crust, for Bountiful
    Pizza, 73
Cedar wraps
    about, 168
    Cedar-Wrapped Halibut with
        Herbed Rice Pilaf, 168
Cheddar cheese, in Southern-
    Style Pesto Shrimp over Cheesy
    Grits, 171

Cheese
    about: as basic pesto
        ingredient, 17
    Crowd-Pleasing Mini Quiches,
        43
    Day after Thanksgiving
        Sandwich, 89
    Fish Tacos with Mango Salsa
        and Pesto Mayo, 175
    Green Eggs and Ham in a
        Shell, 41
    Pesto Omelette Your Way, 44
    Roasted Carrot Bruschetta,
        93
    see also specific cheeses
Chicken
    Easy Baked Parmigiana, 155
    Grilled Pesto Kebabs, 151
    Pesto Fried Rice, 154
    Pesto Noodle Soup, 117
    Pesto-Drizzled Grilled Satay,
        109
    Sizzling Pesto Fajitas, 157
Chinese flavor profiles, 21
Cilantro
    Gazpacho Shooters with
        Pesto Cubes, 114
    Green Shakshuka, 49
    Naan Pizza with Fig and
        Jalapeño Pesto, 66
    Roasted Jalapeño-Cilantro
        Pesto, 30
    Spicy Jalapeño Guacamole, 102
    Spicy Thai-Inspired Noodles,
        55
    Thai-Inspired Pesto
        Vinaigrette, 26
Classic Basil Pesto
    Caprese Salad with Pesto
        Vinaigrette, 134
    Rainbow Pesto Tea
        Sandwiches, 80
    recipe for, 23
    Silky Pesto Goat Cheese
        Terrine, 96
Classic Pesto Vinaigrette
    Pesto-Marinated Swordfish
        Kebabs, 167
    recipe for, 26
Collard greens, in Ultimate
    Veggie Wraps, 137

Compound Pesto Butter
    "Always Make Extra" Potatoes
        with Savory Pesto Butter,
        139
    Buttery Seared Sea Scallops
        over Green Tea Noodles, 165
    Dave's Pesto-Glazed New
        York Strip Steak, 178
    recipe for, 29
    Shrimp Skewers, 110
Cooking methods
    basic, 8-9
    mother sauces and, 12-13
    see also Pesto
Cool Cucumber Bites with Shrimp
    Salad, 98
Corn, in Pesto Minestrone for All
    Seasons, 116
Cotija cheese, in Sizzling Chicken
    Pesto Fajitas, 157
Couscous, Mint Pesto Lamb
    Kebabs with, 192
Cranberry sauce
    about: making quickly, 89
    Day after Thanksgiving
        Sandwich, 89
Cream cheese
    Open-Faced Red Radish and
        Pesto Sandwiches, 81
    Pesto-Stuffed Mushroom
        Caps, 101
    Prosciutto-Wrapped
        Asparagus Spears, 138
Creamy Pesto Hummus
    with Cut Vegetables, 106
    Ultimate Veggie Collard
        Wraps, 137
Crème fraîche, in Green Eggs and
    Ham in a Shell, 41
Crostini
    about: using leftover, 93, 116
    Kale Pesto and Shiitake
        Mushroom, 91
    Roasted Lemon and Pesto, 92
Crowd-Pleasing Mini Quiches, 43
Cubed Butternut Squash over
    Pesto Zucchini Noodles, 140
Cucumber
    Cool Cucumber Bites with
        Shrimp Salad, 98
    Gazpacho Shooters with
        Pesto Cubes, 114

D
Daikon radish noodles, in Spicy
    Thai-Inspired Noodles, 55
Dates
    Butternut Squash Spaghetti,
        143
    Sweet Roasted Date
        Flatbread, 68
Dave's Pesto-Glazed New York
    Strip Steak, 178
Day after Thanksgiving Sandwich,
    89
Devil May Care Eggs, 104
Dice, creating equal-size, 114
Dill pesto alternative, 25
Dressings
    about: vinaigrette contrasted,
        26
    Buttermilk Pesto, 27
    Green Goddess Pesto, 32
    Kale Pesto, 27
    Summer Greens with
        Buttermilk Pesto Dressing,
        132
    Winter Greens with Kale
        Pesto Dressing, 132
    see also Vinaigrettes

E
Edamame, in Pesto Minestrone
    for All Seasons, 116
Eggplant
    Grilled Eggplant Roll-Ups
        with Spicy Pesto Aioli, 100
    Mediterranean Roasted
        Veggie Sandwich, 84
    Ultimate Veggie Collard
        Wraps, 137
Eggs
    about: using large, 6
    Avocado Pesto Toast, 45
    Crowd-Pleasing Mini Quiches,
        43
    Egg Salad and Pesto Tea
        Sandwiches, 81
    Green Eggs and Ham in a
        Shell, 41
    Green Shakshuka, 49
    Leaning Eggplant Towers, 144

Pesto Polenta with Poached
        Eggs in Pepper Rounds, 50
    Red Shakshuka, 49
Eggs, hardboiled
    about, 8
    Devil May Care Eggs, 104
    Pesto Ramen Bowl, 118
    Winter Greens with Kale
        Pesto Dressing, 132
Endive
    Pesto Ramen Bowl, 118
    Summer Greens with Butter-
        milk Pesto Dressing, 132
English cucumber
    Cool Cucumber Bites with
        Shrimp Salad, 98
    Gazpacho Shooters with
        Pesto Cubes, 114
Espagnole, about, 12

F
Fajitas, Sizzling Chicken Pesto,
    157
Fennel
    about: pesto variation, 24
    Cedar-Wrapped Halibut with
        Herbed Rice Pilaf, 168
    Fennel Capellini, 63
    Pesto Sausage Lettuce Wraps,
        189
Feta, in Naan Pizza with Fig and
    Jalapeño Pesto, 66
Figs
    Butternut Squash Spaghetti,
        143
    Naan Pizza with Jalapeño
        Pesto and, 66
Fish
    Cedar-Wrapped Halibut with
        Herbed Rice Pilaf, 168
    Oven-Roasted Pesto-Glazed
        Salmon, 170
    Pesto-Marinated Swordfish
        Kebabs, 167
Flatbread
    Philadelphia Cheese Steak
        Pesto Wraps, 88
    Sweet Roasted Date
        Flatbread, 68
Focaccia rolls, in Mediterranean
    Roasted Veggie Sandwich, 84

Fontina, in Mediterranean Roasted Veggie Sandwich, 84
French flavor profiles, 21
Fried Rice, Chicken Pesto, 154

G

Garlic
about: as optional pesto ingredient, 18; health benefits of, 13
Gazpacho Shooters with Chilled Pesto Cubes, 114
Ginger
Chicken Pesto Fried Rice, 154
Pesto Pork Wonton Soup, 125
Pesto Ramen Bowl, 118
Roasted Carrot and Butternut Squash Soup, 123
Spicy Thai-Inspired Noodles, 55
Goat cheese
Butternut Squash Spaghetti, 143
Open-Faced Cucumber Pesto Sandwiches, 81
Silky Pesto Terrine, 96
Sweet Roasted Date Flatbread, 68
Zucchini Boats Filled with Pesto and, 147
Gouda Goodness BLAT, 82
Green Eggs and Ham in a Shell, 41
Green Goddess Pesto
Green Goddess Pesto Grilled Cheese, 87
recipe for, 32
Green Tea Noodles, Buttery Seared Sea Scallops over, 165
Greens
about: varieties of, 133
Summer Greens with Buttermilk Pesto Dressing, 132
Winter Greens with Kale Pesto Dressing, 132
Grilled Cheese, Green Goddess Pesto, 87
Grilled Eggplant Roll-Ups with Spicy Pesto Aioli, 100
Grits, Southern-Style Pesto Shrimp over Cheesy, 171

Gruyère
Green Eggs and Ham in a Shell, 41
Pesto Omelette Your Way, 44
Pesto-Stuffed Mushroom Caps, 101
Guacamole, Spicy Jalapeño, 102

H

Halibut filets, Cedar-Wrapped, with Herbed Rice Pilaf, 168
Havarti, in Philadelphia Cheese Steak Pesto Wraps, 88
Heartbeet Salad with Orange Honey Mustard Vinaigrette, 129
Herbes de Provence, in Olive Pesto, 32
Herbs
about: herb sauce, 13
Baked Pesto Risotto, 58
Cedar-Wrapped Halibut with Herbed Rice Pilaf, 168
Chicken Pesto Noodle Soup, 117
Creamy Pesto Hummus with Cut Vegetables, 106
Green Shakshuka, 49
Pesto Minestrone for All Seasons, 116
Pesto Omelette Your Way, 44
Red Shakshuka, 49
see also specific herbs
Hollandaise, about, 12
Homemade Croutons
recipe for, 133
Summer Greens with Buttermilk Pesto Dressing, 132
Winter Greens with Kale Pesto Dressing, 132
Hors d'Oeuvres Platter, 110
Hummus
Avocado Pesto, 45
Creamy Pesto, with Cut Vegetables, 106
Mediterranean Roasted Veggie Sandwich, 84
Ultimate Veggie Collard Wraps, 137

I

Indian flavor profiles, 21
Israeli couscous, Mint Pesto Lamb Kebabs with, 192
Italian flavor profiles, 21
Italian sausage, in Pesto Lettuce Wraps, 189

J

Jalapeño
about: 6; roasting of, 9
Gazpacho Shooters with Pesto Cubes, 114
Green Shakshuka, 49
Mango Salsa, 175
Naan Pizza with Fig and Jalapeño Pesto, 66
Roasted Jalapeño-Cilantro Pesto, 30
Spicy Jalapeño Guacamole, 102
Spicy Thai-Inspired Noodles, 55
Jicama, in Summer Greens with Buttermilk Pesto Dressing, 132

K

Kalamata olives
Olive Pesto, 32
Sweet Roasted Date Flatbread, 68
Kale, in Dave's Pesto-Glazed New York Strip Steak, 178
Kale Pesto
Ode to ABC Pizza, 65
Shiitake Mushroom and, Crostini, 91
recipe for, 31
Kale Pesto Dressing
recipe for, 27
Winter Greens with, 132
Kebabs
Grilled Chicken Pesto, 151
Mint Pesto Lamb, with Couscous, 192
Pesto-Marinated Swordfish, 167

L

Lamb, Mint Pesto, Kebabs with Couscous, 192
Lasagna
  about: making lasagna rolls, 56
  Pesto Lasagna, 56
Latin American flavor profiles, 21
Leaning Eggplant Towers, 144
Lemon juice
  about: citrus juices, 6
Lemons, pesto variation, 25
Lettuce
  Gouda Goodness BLAT, 82
  Green Goddess Pesto Grilled Cheese, 87
  Pesto Sausage Wraps, 189
Lime juice
  about: citrus juices, 6

M

Manchego cheese, in Sizzling Chicken Pesto Fajitas, 157
Mango Salsa
  Fish Tacos with Pesto Mayo and, 175
  recipe for, 175
Maple syrup
  Bacon-Wrapped Pesto-Glazed Pork Tenderloin with Roasted Vegetables, 186
  Roasted Carrot and Butternut Squash Soup, 123
  Roasted Carrot Bruschetta, 93
Mascarpone, in Butternut Squash Ravioli with Pesto Sauce, 59
Mediterranean Roasted Veggie Sandwich, 84
Meyer lemons
  Cedar-Wrapped Halibut with Herbed Rice Pilaf, 168
  Roasted Lemon and Pesto Crostini, 92
Middle Eastern flavor profiles, 21
Milk, about, 6
Minestrone, Pesto, for All Seasons, 116
Mint Pesto

Lamb Kebabs with Couscous, 192
Philadelphia Cheese Steak Pesto Wraps, 88
recipe for, 31
Mother sauces, 12-13
Mozzarella cheese
  Bountiful Cauliflower Crust Pizza, 73
  Caprese Calzone, 74
  Caprese Salad with Pesto Vinaigrette, 134
  Caprese Skewers, 110
  Easy Baked Chicken Parmigiana, 155
  Leaning Eggplant Towers, 144
  Ode to ABC Pizza, 65
  Pesto Lasagna, 56
  Tortellini Skewers, 110
Mushrooms
  Bountiful Cauliflower Crust Pizza, 73
  Green Shakshuka, 49
  Kale Pesto and Shiitake Mushroom Crostini, 91
  Pesto Ramen Bowl, 118
  Pesto-Marinated Swordfish Kebabs, 167
  Pesto-Stuffed Mushroom Caps, 101
Mustard
  Devil May Care Eggs, 105
  Easy Baked Chicken Parmigiana, 155
  Orange Honey Mustard Vinaigrette, 129
  Spicy Pesto Aioli, 27

N

Naan Pizza with Fig and Jalapeño Pesto, 66
Noodles, in Chicken Pesto Soup, 117
Nuts
  about: as basic pesto ingredient, 18; toasting of, 9
  Candied, in Cubed Butternut Squash over Pesto Zucchini Noodles, 140
  see also specific nuts

O

Ode to ABC Pizza, 65
Oil, as basic pesto ingredient, 17
Olive oil, about, 6
Olives
  Olive Pesto, 32
  Rainbow Pesto Tea Sandwiches, 80
  Sweet Roasted Date Flatbread, 68
  Tortellini Skewers, 110
Omelettes
  about: two methods for making, 44
  Pesto Omelette Your Way, 44
"One and Done" Chicken and Veggie Plate, 158
Onions
  about, 6
Open-faced sandwiches
  Cucumber Pesto, 81
  Red Radish and Pesto, 81
  Smoked Salmon Pesto, 81
Orange Honey Mustard Vinaigrette
  Heartbeet Salad with, 129
  recipe for, 129
Oranges, in Heartbeet Salad with Orange Honey Mustard Vinaigrette, 129
Orecchiette, Roasted Broccoli, 62
Orzo, in Pesto Minestrone for All Seasons, 116
Oven-Roasted Pesto-Glazed Salmon, 170

P

Pancetta
  Bountiful Cauliflower Crust Pizza, 73
  Butternut Squash Spaghetti, 143
  Ode to ABC Pizza, 65
Pantry primer, 7
Pappardelle, Roasted Beet and Blood Orange, 63
Paprika, about, 6
Parmesan cheese
  Baked Pesto Risotto, 58

Bountiful Cauliflower Crust Pizza, 73
Butternut Squash Ravioli with Pesto Sauce, 59
Buttery Seared Sea Scallops over Green Tea Noodles, 165
Easy Baked Chicken Parmigiana, 155
Pesto Polenta with Poached Eggs in Pepper Rounds, 50
Pesto Turkey Meatballs with Tomato Sauce, 160-161
Parmigiano Reggiano
    about: as basic pesto ingredient, 17; health benefits of, 13
    Classic Basil Pesto, 23
    Green Goddess Pesto, 32
    Kale Pesto, 31
    Kale Pesto and Shiitake Mushroom Crostini, 91
    Ode to ABC Pizza, 65
    Roasted Jalapeño-Cilantro Pesto, 30
    Sun-Dried Tomato Pesto, 30
Parsley
    about: pesto variation, 25
    Crowd-Pleasing Mini Quiches, 43
    Green Goddess Pesto, 32
    Mint Pesto, 31
    Naan Pizza with Fig and Jalapeño Pesto, 66
    Pesto Minestrone for All Seasons, 116
    Pesto Turkey Meatballs with Tomato Sauce, 160
    see also Herbs
Pasta
    about: reserving water from cooking of, 6
    Butternut Squash Spaghetti, 143
    Chicken Pesto Noodle Soup, 117
    Fennel Capellini, 63
    Leaning Eggplant Towers, 144
    Pasta Trilogy, 62-63
    Pesto Turkey Meatballs with Tomato Sauce, 160-161
    Spicy Thai-Inspired Noodles, 55

Peanuts, in Spicy Thai-Inspired Noodles, 55
Pearl onions, in Pesto-Marinated Swordfish Kebabs, 167
Peas, in Mint Pesto, 31
Pepper sauce, about, 13
Peppercorns, Tellicherry, 6
Pesto, 4, 13
    basic ingredients of, 6, 5-19
    making in advance, 4
    mise en place method for cooking, 4
    pantry recommendations, 7
    preserving of, 20
    recipe variations, 21
    using up leftover, 20
    varieties of, 24-25
    worksheets for making varieties of, 199-201
Pesto Cream-Filled Flank Steak Roulade, 182
Pesto Crostini and Bruschetta Party, 91-93
Pesto Cubes, Gazpacho Shooters with Chilled, 114
Pesto Lasagna, 56
Pesto Mayo
    Day after Thanksgiving Sandwich, 89
    Easy Baked Chicken Parmigiana, 155
    Fish Tacos with Mango Salsa and, 175
    Mediterranean Roasted Veggie Sandwich, 84
    Pesto-Stuffed Burgers, 180
    recipe for, 27
Pesto Minestrone for All Seasons, 116
Pesto Omelette Your Way, 44
Pesto Pasta Trilogy, 62-63
Pesto Polenta with Poached Eggs in Pepper Rounds, 50
Pesto Pork Wonton Soup, 125
Pesto Quinoa-Stuffed Roasted Red Peppers, 146
Pesto Ramen Bowl, 118
Pesto Sausage Lettuce Wraps, 189
Pesto Shakshuka, Green and Red, 48-49

Pesto Turkey Meatballs with Tomato Sauce, 160-161
Pesto-Drizzled Grilled Chicken Satay, 109
Pesto-Marinated Swordfish Kebabs, 167
Pesto-Stuffed Burgers, 180
Pesto-Stuffed Mushroom Caps, 101
Philadelphia Cheese Steak Pesto Wraps, 88
Pie crust, for Crowd-Pleasing Mini Quiches, 43
Pine nuts
    about: as basic pesto ingredient, 18; health benefits of, 13
    Classic Basil Pesto, 23
    Roasted Jalapeño-Cilantro Pesto, 30
Pistachios
    Green Goddess Pesto, 32
    Heartbeet Salad with Orange Honey Mustard Vinaigrette, 129
    Mint Pesto Lamb Kebabs with Couscous, 192
Pizza
    Bountiful Cauliflower Crust Pizza, 73
    Naan Pizza with Fig and Jalapeño Pesto, 66
    Ode to ABC Pizza, 65
Plants, as basic pesto ingredient, 16
Polenta, Pesto, with Poached Eggs in Pepper Rounds, 50
Pork
    Bacon-Wrapped Pesto-Glazed Tenderloin with Roasted Vegetables, 186
    Pesto Pork Wonton Soup, 125
    Pesto Sausage Lettuce Wraps, 189
Potatoes
    "Always Make Extra" Potatoes with Savory Pesto Butter, 139
    Bacon-Wrapped Pesto-Glazed Pork Tenderloin with Roasted Vegetables, 186

Chicken Pesto Noodle Soup, 117

"One and Done" Chicken and Veggie Plate, 158

Pesto Cream-Filled Flank Steak Roulade, 182

Pesto Minestrone for All Seasons, 116

Roasted Broccoli Potato Soup, 123

Prosciutto
Pesto Cream-Filled Flank Steak Roulade, 182
Prosciutto-Wrapped Asparagus Spears, 138
Sweet Roasted Date Flatbread, 68

Provolone
Green Goddess Pesto Grilled Cheese, 87
Pesto Cream-Filled Flank Steak Roulade, 182

Puff pastry, for Green Eggs and Ham in a Shell, 41

Q

Quiches, Crowd-Pleasing Mini, 43

Quinoa
Pesto Quinoa-Stuffed Roasted Red Peppers, 146
Ultimate Veggie Collard Wraps, 137

R

Radishes
Open-Faced Red Radish and Pesto Sandwiches, 81
Summer Greens with Buttermilk Pesto Dressing, 132
Ultimate Veggie Collard Wraps, 137

Rainbow Pesto Tea Sandwiches, 80

Raisins, in Mint Pesto Lamb Kebabs with Couscous, 192

Ramen noodles, in Pesto Ramen Bowl, 118

Ravioli
about: preparing in advance, 59
Butternut Squash Ravioli with Pesto Sauce, 59

Red Shakshuka, 49

Rice
about: cooking of, 8
Baked Pesto Risotto, 58
Cedar-Wrapped Halibut with Herbed Rice Pilaf, 168
Chicken Pesto Fried Rice, 154
Pesto Sausage Lettuce Wraps, 189

Ricotta
Avocado Ricotta Pesto, 45
Bountiful Cauliflower Crust Pizza, 73
Grilled Eggplant Roll-Ups with Spicy Pesto Aioli, 100
Ode to ABC Pizza, 65
Pesto Lasagna, 56
Pesto Turkey Meatballs with Tomato Sauce, 160-161

Risotto, Baked Pesto, 58

Roasted Beet and Bean Soup, 124

Roasted Beet and Blood Orange Pappardelle, 63

Roasted Broccoli Orecchiette, 62

Roasted Broccoli Potato Soup, 123

Roasted Carrot and Butternut Squash Soup, 123

Roasted Carrot Bruschetta, 93

Roasted Jalapeño-Cilantro Pesto
Rainbow Pesto Tea Sandwiches, 80
recipe for, 30
Silky Pesto Goat Cheese Terrine, 96
Spicy Jalapeño Guacamole, 102

Roasted Lemon and Pesto Crostini, 92

S

Salads
about: tips for making, 133
Caprese Salad with Pesto Vinaigrette, 134
Heartbeet Salad with Orange Honey Mustard Vinaigrette, 129
Summer Greens with Buttermilk Pesto Dressing, 132
Winter Greens with Kale Pesto Dressing, 132

Salmon, Oven-Roasted Pesto-Glazed, 170

Salt, about, 6

Sandwiches
Day after Thanksgiving Sandwich, 89
Egg Salad and Pesto Tea Sandwiches, 81
Green Goddess Pesto Grilled Cheese, 87
Gouda Goodness BLAT, 82
Mediterranean Roasted Veggie Sandwich, 84
Open-Faced Cucumber Pesto Sandwiches, 81
Open-Faced Red Radish and Pesto Sandwiches, 81
Open-Faced Smoked Salmon Pesto Sandwiches, 81
Rainbow Pesto Tea Sandwiches, 80

Sausage
Italian, in Pesto Sausage Lettuce Wraps, 189
pork, in Pesto Pork Wonton Soup, 125

Scallions
about, 6
Butternut Squash Ravioli with Pesto Sauce, 59
Chicken Pesto Fried Rice, 154
Crowd-Pleasing Mini Quiches, 43
Devil May Care Eggs, 104
Mint Pesto, 31
Pesto Minestrone for All Seasons, 116
Pesto Omelette Your Way, 44
Pesto Pork Wonton Soup, 125
Pesto Ramen Bowl, 118
Pesto Turkey Meatballs with Tomato Sauce, 160-161
Spicy Jalapeño Guacamole, 102
Spicy Thai-Inspired Noodles, 55

Scallops, Buttery Seared Sea, over Green Tea Noodles, 165

Seasonings, as basic pesto ingredient, 19
Shakshuka
  about, 49
  Green, 49
  Red, 49
Shallots
  Dave's Pesto-Glazed New York Strip Steak, 178
  Kale Pesto, 31
  Pesto Minestrone for All Seasons, 116
  Pesto Pork Wonton Soup, 125
Shrimp
  about: poaching of, 98
  Cool Cucumber Bites with Shrimp Salad, 98
  Shrimp Skewers, 110
  Southern-Style Pesto Shrimp over Cheesy Grits, 171
  Spicy Pesto Shrimp Bruschetta, 93
Silky Pesto Goat Cheese Terrine, 96
Sizzling Chicken Pesto Fajitas, 157
Skewered Hors d'Oeuvres Platter, 110
Smoked salmon
  Avocado Pesto Toast, 45
  Open-Faced Pesto Sandwiches, 81
Sour cream
  Butternut Squash Ravioli with Pesto Sauce, 59
  Pesto Cream-Filled Flank Steak Roulade, 182
Southern-Style Shrimp over Cheesy Grits, 171
Soy sauce
  Pesto Pork Wonton Soup, 125
  Pesto Ramen Bowl, 118
Spaghetti
  Butternut Squash, 143
  Pesto Turkey Meatballs with Tomato Sauce, 160-161
Spicy Jalapeño Guacamole, 102
Spicy Pesto Aioli
  Grilled Eggplant Roll-Ups with, 100
  recipe for, 27
  Sizzling Chicken Pesto Fajitas, 157

Spicy Pesto Shrimp Bruschetta, 93
Spicy Thai-Inspired Noodles, 55
Spinach
  about: pesto variation, 25
  Green Shakshuka, 49
  Pesto Turkey Meatballs with Tomato Sauce, 160-161
Spiralizing, of vegetables
  about, 9, 140
  Butternut Squash Spaghetti, 143
  Spicy Thai-Inspired Noodles, 55
Strawberries, in Caprese Salad with Pesto Vinaigrette, 134
Sugar, about, 6
Sugar snap peas
  Pesto Minestrone for All Seasons, 116
  Spicy Thai-Inspired Noodles, 55
Summer Greens with Buttermilk Pesto Dressing, 129
Sun-Dried Tomato Pesto
  Grilled Chicken Pesto Kebabs, 151
  Rainbow Pesto Tea Sandwiches, 80
  recipe for, 30
  Red Shakshuka, 49
  Silky Pesto Goat Cheese Terrine, 96
  Sizzling Chicken Pesto Fajitas, 157
  Spicy Pesto Shrimp Bruschetta, 93
Sun-dried tomatoes
  Olive Pesto, 32
  Sun-Dried Tomato Pesto, 30
Sweet Roasted Date Flatbread, 68
Swiss cheese, in Crowd-Pleasing Mini Quiches, 43
Swordfish steaks, in Pesto-Marinated Kebabs, 167

T

Tacos, Fish, with Mango Salsa and Pesto Mayo, 175

Tahini
  about, 13, 106
  Creamy Pesto Hummus with Cut Vegetables, 106
Tangy Pesto Vinaigrette
  "One and Done" Chicken and Veggie Plate, 158
  recipe for, 26
Tarragon, in Green Goddess Pesto, 32
Tea Sandwiches, 79-81
Terrine, Silky Pesto Goat Cheese, 96
Thai flavor profiles, 21
Thai-Inspired Pesto
  Pesto-Drizzled Grilled Chicken Satay, 109
  Thai-Inspired Pesto Vinaigrette, 26
Thai-Inspired Pesto Vinaigrette
  recipe for, 26
  Spicy Thai-Inspired Noodles, 55
Toast, Avocado Pesto, 45
Tofu, in Spicy Thai-Inspired Noodles, 55
Tomat, about, 12
Tomato Sauce
  Caprese Calzone, 74
  Pesto Lasagna, 56
  Pesto Turkey Meatballs with, 160-161
  recipe for, 161
Tomatoes, canned
  Red Shakshuka, 49
  Tomato Sauce, 161
Tomatoes, cherry
  Caprese Salad with Pesto Vinaigrette, 134
  Caprese Skewers, 110
  Grilled Chicken Pesto Kebabs, 151
  Leaning Eggplant Towers, 144
  "One and Done" Chicken and Veggie Plate, 158
  Rainbow Pesto Tea Sandwiches, 80
Tomatoes, fresh
  Crowd-Pleasing Mini Quiches, 43
  Gazpacho Shooters with Pesto Cubes, 114

Gouda Goodness BLAT, 82
Leaning Eggplant Towers, 144
Tomatoes, green
Green Goddess Pesto Grilled
Cheese, 87
Green Shakshuka, 49
Tortellini Skewers, 110
Tortillas
Fish Tacos with Mango Salsa
and Pesto Mayo, 175
Sizzling Chicken Pesto Fajitas,
157
Tri-Color Roasted Veggie Soup
Bar, 122-124
Turbinado sugar
about, 6
Sun-Dried Tomato Pesto, 30
Turkey
Day after Thanksgiving
Sandwich, 89
Pesto Turkey Meatballs with
Tomato Sauce, 160-161

U

Ultimate Veggie Collard Wraps,
137

V

Vegetable broth
Baked Pesto Risotto, 58
Pesto Polenta with Poached
Eggs in Pepper Rounds, 50
Pesto Pork Wonton Soup, 125
Pesto Quinoa-Stuffed
Roasted Red Peppers, 146

Pesto Ramen Bowl, 118
Roasted Beet and Bean Soup,
124
Roasted Broccoli Potato
Soup, 123
Roasted Carrot and Butternut
Squash Soup, 123
Southern-Style Pesto Shrimp
over Cheesy Grits, 171
Vegetables
about: spiralizing of, 9, 40
Creamy Pesto Hummus with
Cut Vegetables, 106
Green Eggs and Ham in a
Shell, 41
Mediterranean Roasted
Veggie Sandwich, 84
Ultimate Veggie Collard
Wraps, 137
see also specific vegetables
Velouté, about, 12
Vinaigrettes
about: dressing contrasted,
26
Classic Pesto, 26
Heartbeet Salad with Orange
Honey Mustard, 129
Orange Honey Mustard, 129
Tangy Pesto, 26
Thai-Inspired Pesto, 26

W

White fish, in Tacos with Mango
Salsa and Pesto Mayo, 175
Winter Greens with Kale Pesto
Dressing, 132

Wonton wrappers
about: preparing in advance,
125
Butternut Squash Ravioli with
Pesto Sauce, 59
Pesto Pork Wonton Soup, 125

Y

Yellow squash
Grilled Chicken Pesto Kebabs,
151
"One and Done" Chicken and
Veggie Plate, 158
Yogurt
about, 13
Mint Pesto Lamb Kebabs with
Couscous, 192
Philadelphia Cheese Steak
Pesto Wraps, 88

Z

Zucchini
Cubed Butternut Squash over
Zucchini Noodles, 140
Grilled Chicken Pesto Kebabs,
151
Mediterranean Roasted
Veggie Sandwich, 84
"One and Done" Chicken and
Veggie Plate, 158
Ultimate Veggie Collard
Wraps, 137
Zucchini Boats Filled with
Pesto and Goat Cheese, 147

About the Author

Leslie Derene Lennox is a recipe developer, cooking instructor, urban gardener, and the founder of Hope's Gardens, an artisan condiment company based in Atlanta. A former fashion stylist in New York and Los Angeles, she worked with Vera Wang at *Vogue*, spent time as an art photographer, and founded a hand-crafted products and greeting card company, selling her designs internationally through Barneys, Papyrus, and many other fine retailers. She has always had a talent for making inspired, resourceful creations with what is at hand. Today, Leslie lives in New York City with her husband, Dave, and their two kitties, Spirit and Max. *Pesto: The Modern Mother Sauce* is her first cookbook. Find out more on Instagram (@hopesgardenspesto) and at hopesgardens.com.